SO-AQN-292

THE DEVIL IS IN THE
DETAILS

THE DEVIL IS IN THE
DETAILS

System Solutions for Equity, Excellence, and Student Well-Being

MICHAEL FULLAN

MARY JEAN GALLAGHER

FOR INFORMATION:

Corwin

A SAGE Company

2455 Teller Road

Thousand Oaks, California 91320

(800) 233-9936

www.corwin.com

SAGE Publications Ltd.

1 Oliver's Yard

55 City Road

London EC1Y 1SP

United Kingdom

SAGE Publications India Pvt. Ltd.

B 1/I 1 Mohan Cooperative Industrial Area

Mathura Road, New Delhi 110 044

India

SAGE Publications Asia-Pacific Pte. Ltd.

18 Cross Street #10-10/11/12

China Square Central

Singapore 048423

Publisher: Arnis Burvikovs

Acquisitions Editor: Ariel Curry

Development Editor: Desirée A. Bartlett

Associate Editor: Eliza B. Erickson

Production Editor: Melanie Birdsall

Copy Editor: Lynne Curry

Typesetter: C&M Digitals (P) Ltd.

Proofreader: Lawrence W. Baker

Indexer: Molly Hall

Cover Designer: Janet Kiesel

Marketing Manager: Sharon Pendergast

Copyright © 2020 by Corwin Press, Inc.

All rights reserved. Except as permitted by U.S. copyright law, no part of this work may be reproduced or distributed in any form or by any means, or stored in a database or retrieval system, without permission in writing from the publisher.

When forms and sample documents appearing in this work are intended for reproduction, they will be marked as such. Reproduction of their use is authorized for educational use by educators, local school sites, and/or noncommercial or nonprofit entities that have purchased the book.

All third-party trademarks referenced or depicted herein are included solely for the purpose of illustration and are the property of their respective owners. Reference to these trademarks in no way indicates any relationship with, or endorsement by, the trademark owner.

Printed in Canada

ISBN 978-1-5443-1797-7

This book is printed on acid-free paper.

20 21 22 23 24 10 9 8 7 6 5 4 3 2 1

DISCLAIMER: This book may direct you to access third-party content via web links, QR codes, or other scannable technologies, which are provided for your reference by the author(s). Corwin makes no guarantee that such third-party content will be available for your use and encourages you to review the terms and conditions of such third-party content. Corwin takes no responsibility and assumes no liability for your use of any third-party content, nor does Corwin approve, sponsor, endorse, verify, or certify such third-party content.

Contents

We will argue that the world is heading into the jaws of mass extinction or radical decline of human existence. Whether it will take 20 or 100 years remains to be seen. We need a new moral imperative *and* a system transformation strategy that goes along with it to have any chance of surviving for the better. The moral imperative with the help of education is "to become better at learning and better at life," which we will spell out in subsequent chapters. This moral imperative will need to be both an individual and a collective phenomenon. In essence this means that whatever level of the system you are at you will need:

a. To understand your own level and that of your peers.

b. To gain greater understanding of each of the other two levels.

c. And to work accordingly toward greater equity, excellence, and well-being that in turn favors becoming "good at life."

For the past 20 years and more, we have been students and promoters of system change in education. We have helped to lead change in direct attempts to achieve whole system improvement. In Ontario, Canada, Michael Fullan was policy adviser to two successive premiers from 2003 to 2018. Within that same period (2008–2015), Mary Jean Gallagher was assistant deputy minister in the province charged with leading the learning transformation in the 4,900 schools and 72 districts involving two million students in the province. If you like, Fullan was the external change agent and Gallagher the internal change agent. For the past six years we have worked on two other whole system change initiatives: California in the United States with its 10,700 schools, 1,009 districts, 58 counties, and over six million students; and the state of Victoria in Australia (1,560 schools). All three cases involved deliberate, successful-to-a-point policies and action intended to improve the whole system (two of the three, California and Victoria, are continuing to evolve the policies that they began with; Ontario has stalled due to a change in government in 2018).

At the same time, we have consulted with or studied numerous other systems around the world as well as immersed ourselves in the research and practice literature on educational change. As we consider system change for 2020 and beyond, we have the sense that we are at a particular time in history where dramatic change is in the cards—for better or for worse. More and more of us, including some policy makers, have concluded that the approaches used over the past two decades have increasingly failed to work; that the world is in a crisis not encountered for hundreds and maybe thousands of years; that there are glimpses of what should be done; and that young people are our greatest hope. Is it possible to liberate the system while maintaining focus? This book will take you on such a journey.

Part I

....

System Change

The two chapters in Part I set the stage for the book.

Chapter 1, The Nature of the Beast, examines three big change forces: the march of evolution; the dramatic toll of rising inequity; and the serious deficiency of current policies. Although the average citizen cannot do much directly about these mighty societal factors, to know them is to understand the context within which we live and the trends that will affect our immediate future. To appreciate evolution is to realize how humankind has become so magnificent as a species, while acquiring the power to self-destruct. Social awareness and attraction to others can be one of humankind's greatest natural assets. Cooperation and teamwork have resulted in prodigious accomplishments. Or they can lead to tribalism, distrust, deadly conflict between groups. The message to the reader is to help tip the balance in favor of collaboration on an ever-wider scale, not just in our own local circles. If the three forces—social evolution, greater equity, and better policies—can be channeled into future developments, we have a chance of overcoming the status quo, which we argue will not end well if allowed to persist.

Chapter 2, The Emergence of System Solutions, begins to map out how we might tackle the dangerous state of the status quo in order to create a better future through *coordinated system change*. We need to do this by taking the following steps: (a) realizing the limits of complex solutions in favor of strategies that mobilize people at all three levels of the system—local, middle, and macro; and (b) appreciating and cultivating the *phenomenology of good system change*—that is, by understanding the worldview of those at each of the three levels of the system, and by strengthening mutual understandings of people across the levels. In essence, this means understanding one's own and others' *context*—the details and nature of everyday lives—and (c) developing an appreciation of a new form of system change in which systems operate in a combination of upward proactivity (to other levels), downward liberation and facilitation, and lateral learning within each level (see Chapter 2, Figure 2.2).

Part I provides a springboard to successful system action across the three levels that we take up in Part II.

1

The Nature of the Beast

. . . .

It's turtles all the way down.

—An infinite regression anecdote
cited by Stephen Hawking

This chapter is not a treatise on system change per se. We won't be taking the reader into any abstract theoretical discussion. The moment you do that is the moment you lose the plot, which is *What can ordinary people—all people, really—do to reflect system thinking in their daily existence?* The latter is the only hope for practical system change to have a proactive and ubiquitous presence and thus make the profound difference that will be required for survival of the human race.

If you stay at the abstract level, it is easy to get bogged down, hopelessly confused, and end up with a sense of the surreal. You can carefully examine descriptions of "system thinking" and of "complexity theory" and still not know what each means let alone their relationship to each other and to practical matters. Both theories address hidden forces, interdependencies, nonlinear developments, continuous feedback, complex adaptive responses, negative consequences for the environment, and much more. If you *study* these theories—say, do a doctoral dissertation on the topic—you will end up with very few people who want to talk with you. Yet understanding and influencing system change is crucial to the very future of humankind. The question then, and our goal in this book, is to make system thinking available to the average person— essentially how to better understand and influence the dynamics of change within and across the three levels of the system.

> Our goal is to make system thinking accessible to the average person.

We get at system dynamics in education inside the practicalities of working with all levels and all ages of those within the system. It turns out that "leading practitioners" are system players even if they don't know it explicitly. So, here is our main proposition for this book: Whatever level of the system you operate in, you need to become expert practitioners in working with systems and members at all levels therein, indeed in leading others to do the same. Our message is that you must immerse yourself in action and reflective practice. Learning complex things takes us to the heart of how change best occurs among humans. It usually is not through some cognitive breakthrough (aha, I've got it), but rather through new *experiences that cause us to ask new questions.* We know from neuroscience in the past decade that new things that "stick" with us are a result of episodes that touch us *emotionally.* If these happenings are social in nature, they become all the more powerful because people reinforce and extend each other in groups. As we proceed in this fashion, we can *then* make sense of our learning cognitively. Here is the deal then: Because we build our theory from the ground up in interaction with practitioners of all ages and at all levels, we can guarantee that you will know more about systems theory after reading, thinking, and trying out the ideas in this book than if you spend triple the time studying systems theory. And your learning will be distinctly practical;

you will become more effective in leading and creating improved learning for students across the system. We are being pedagogically playful here. You should do both—make theory and practice a two-way street.

In the course of the chapters, we will examine how system dynamics play themselves out and what this means for how we should address them by way of policy, strategy, and everyday practice. In this chapter we take up the fundamental question of why changes in the status quo are fundamental to our future and the existence of the planet. We identify the forces that may in combination provide the power to overcome our most formidable obstacle: the inertia of the status quo.

In Chapter 2 we identify some of the practical language of system thinking in order to get at detail in ways that leverage system change. This will set us up for Part II where we delve into the system at each of its three main levels and their interaction: local, middle, and macro.

The first key question in Chapter 2 is "Are there more forces potentially in favor of positive change compared to forces preserving the status quo?" If the answer to that question is yes, we would suggest that the lack of systemic thinking is getting in the way of bringing about changes that people actually desire or would embrace upon experiencing it. This would then take us to identifying the practicalities of systemic forces that would move education forward. At the present moment, in our view, the world may be evolving to a state that the majority of people on the planet do not desire.

We want also to say that no system in the world has solved the problem of achieving ongoing system change and improvement—not Finland, not Singapore, not anyone. In fact, the world is currently losing ground relative to educational success, as we will show in this chapter. Moreover, more and more policy makers are realizing that current strategies are not working. In this sense they are more open to alternatives. Our book is intended to provide a new and potentially more powerful alternative for moving forward into 2020 and beyond.

The times resonate well with the Canadian poet and songwriter Leonard Cohen's 1992 song "Anthem": "Ring the bells that still can ring. . . . There is a crack, a crack in everything. That's how the light gets in."

We will see in Part II that there are systems, big ones like California, that have given up on the bells that have stopped or never did ring and are now leveraging the cracks of light that are shining on systems than can work.

Just over 25 years later (2018), on his birthday and just before he died, Cohen lamented that no light was getting in. His haunting song "You Want It Darker" speaks of hopelessness and "We kill the flame" despite "a million candles burning" represents a state of despair.

In this chapter we do flirt with disaster as we consider three big reasons why we need a system perspective to face off with the devil: (1) evolution should worry us; (2) inequity is reaching dangerous heights; and (3) current policies are woefully inadequate. In each case and in combination, we will see that large numbers of people at *all socioeconomic status (SES) levels* are realizing that humanity is steadily losing ground to powerful negative forces. Many people, especially the young, are desperately seeking a solution and are willing to fight for it.

If turned in positive directions, the three forces—evolution, equity, and better policies—could combine to halt and reverse the decline that we are so dangerously living through. Or, if left alone, they could be the end of us. The future could go either way—thrive or dive.

Three Reasons for Adopting a Systems Perspective

Adopting a system perspective will enable us to address

1. The current trajectory of evolution

2. Actions to combat inequity and increase equity in society as a whole

3. Actions to improve policies to strengthen systems as a whole

THE MARCH OF EVOLUTION

Drawing on the empirical findings of leading evolutionary biologists, especially E. O. Wilson (2014), D. S. Wilson (2019), and neuroscientist Damasio (2018), and our own and others, work in the "humanities," we lay out the case that the human race is getting increasingly close to a tipping point that could go either way: toward flourishing or radical decline. Right now, given inertia and lack of capacity to act collectively, the odds favor extinction.

The argument is complex but not difficult to amass and understand:

1.   Humans do not have a special place in the universe; we "lucked out" due to evolutionary developments that ended up privileging us with big brains and capacity therein.

2.   Humans are not intrinsically good. Each of us is conflicted; sometimes we are selfish, other times committing to others and the common good (only sociopaths—about 4% of the population—are oblivious to good). We may have tendencies to cooperate and favor mutual help, but only if certain conditions prevail. We believe that "goodness" has the edge, but it needs certain conditions to win out. Hence our book.

3.   We are social beings born to connect: We have "inherited propensities to communicate, recognize and evaluate, bond, cooperate, compete, and from all these, the deep warm pleasure of belonging to our own special group" (E. O. Wilson, 2014, p. 75). BUT, this can just as easily take the form of "tribalism"—my group is good; all others are bad or irrelevant.

4.   Building on number 3, D. S. Wilson (2019) states: "Modern evolutionary theory tells us that goodness *can* evolve, but only when special conditions are met. That's why we must become wise managers of evolutionary processes. Otherwise evolution takes us where we don't want to go" (pp. 13–14). Yes, goodness "can" evolve, but only under certain conditions. We are optimists and believe that humankind is tipped in favor of positive conditions. Stated differently, when conditions worsen, "system thinking" is more likely to be on the rise because people take to the big picture more readily when the need is evident. Our book is about how goodness can evolve.

5.   "This means that an evolving population is not just a population of individuals, but also a population of *groups*. If individuals vary in their propensity for good and evil, then this variation will exist at two levels: variation among individuals within groups, and variation among groups within the entire population" (D. S. Wilson, 2019, p. 77).

6.   Damasio claims that "so far" evolution "has guided nonconsciously and non-deliberately, without prior design, the selection of biological structures and mechanisms capable of not only maintaining but also advancing the evolution of the species" (p. 26). Notice the qualification "so far."

7.   Our invisible fortune (as just mentioned in number six) may be running out for two reasons. One is Damasio's claim that things are becoming much more complex to a point where destructive forces may prevail. The second reason is that humans have now reached a level of sophistication that they can intervene in biological evolution, such as with clones, artificial intelligence (AI), or extending life. Further, these interventions likely have unknown evolutionary consequences. There is no reason to believe that by themselves AI and its associates will favor humankind—if anything just the opposite (see point nine below).

8.   While humans are born to connect to other humans, this does not apply (except for a few of us and for many indigenous populations) to Mother Nature and the universe—the latter to most of us are not "living things" in the same way other humans are. This fact alone and our neglect of the nonhuman but living universe could be the end of us. Humans have arrogantly and naively become self-appointed godlike rulers of the universe. "We have become the mind of the planet and perhaps our corner of the galaxy as well. We can do with Earth what we please. We chatter constantly about destroying it—by nuclear war, climate change . . ." (E. O. Wilson, 2014, p. 176).

9.   There are other forces at play such as climate change and technology that are part and parcel of evolution. Climate change is perilously close to destroying the planet and large swaths of humans with it. More broadly, don't expect technology to do us any favors. It has a life of its own and for every marvelous invention there is the basic growing realization that "no one is in charge." A former Google strategist and Oxford-trained philosopher, Williams (2019) argues persuasively that technology has robbed us of one of the greatest natural resources that humans have: the capacity to *pay attention*. "Information abundance consumes attention" observes Williams, leaving little time to think (p. 15). He concludes that the "liberation of attention may be the defining moral and political struggle of our time" (p. xii). Further, there is "a deep misalignment between the goals we have for ourselves, and the goals our technologies have for us" (p. 9). The more our attention is consumed, the less prudent we become, argues Williams: "Sometimes the struggle to see what is in front of your nose is the struggle to get away from it so you can see the whole" (p. 12).

More worries: Thomas Siebel, CEO of a company that provides artificial intelligence software, captures the latest developments of digital transformation with a book that has the ironic subtitle *Survive and Thrive in an Era of Mass Extinction* (Siebel, 2019). He then proceeds to describe the core of digital transformation as "the confluence of four profoundly disruptive technologies—cloud computing, big data, the internet of things (IoT), and artificial intelligence" (p. 9). Siebel concludes that these digital transformations "can unlock tremendous economic value, and competitive benefits" (p. 209). But for the life of us we could not find the words "human" or "social" in the entire book. Anytime you get powerful forces with no humans in the equation, start running for cover!

This is where evolution is taking us when we don't have time to pay attention. The solutions will have to be systemic. In the past we could count on evolution and the comparative simplicity of social interaction to resolve these issues in our long-term favor. *This is no longer the case.* It is too complex, too unpredictable, and too susceptible to arbitrary intervention by humans acting as idiosyncratic agents. As Damasio puts it, given our more complex evolution and intervention therein, "To expect *spontaneous* homeostatic harmony from large and cacophonous human collectives is to expect the unlikely" (p. 219, italics in original). If we can no longer depend on "spontaneous" solutions, it is time to deliberately try and shape the future for the better.

We are not talking about one country getting better here and there. True to our system principles, the solutions concern systems within systems that are interdependent. System thinking for Senge and others has always been about *sustainability* under ever complex, multivariate conditions. The biochemist Leslie Orgel's Second Rule is "Evolution is cleverer than you are"—meaning that random variations seeking adaptive solutions will find solutions that humans would not have discovered. True enough—*so far*— but humans are now tampering with gene manipulation and enabling technology to run rampant in a way that may alter future trajectories for the worse. Thus, the question becomes: Can we position ourselves to fashion education as a force for tweaking evolution in a positive direction? We will need systemic thinking to do that. We will need a new kind of education system—one that features equity, excellence, and well-being.

So, one big force for change increasingly obvious to people of all ages is evolution. Up to this point those who have studied or thought about evolution have assumed that it eventually is a good thing (Damasio's "without prior design [has ended up] favoring the species"). Our point in this book is that the forces are so complex, dynamic, and fraught with danger that we can no longer assume that good outcomes are guaranteed.

We like Andres Campero's (2019) treatment of human evolution because of its comprehensive simplicity. Campero states that we can boil down our complexity to the interaction of three fundamental forces: genes, culture, and consciousness. *Genes* are molecules and patterns of molecules that have evolved over time through adaptation to ever-complex environments. Genes are at the core of many of our instinctive actions and desires. They are a result of a long process of "chemical evolution" that led to complex molecules resulting eventually to become our evolving DNAs.

Cultures refer to the customs and habits of groups and subgroups that derived from rudimentary and eventually sophisticated forms of communication and interaction. At some point, claims Campero (2019), "cultural evolution started to become intertwined with genetic evolution thus changing the evolutionary landscape" (p. 34). *Consciousness* is the mystery. Where did it come from? If it's a chemical process, when and how did it first emerge? Genes and culture exist independent of consciousness. Even though we can describe and internalize cultures, they originate and exist mostly outside our consciousness.

Where does this take us with respect to the present and near future? For one thing, we are at the point of consciousness and knowledge where "we can decide which genes we want to eliminate and repress," and because "evolution is cleverer than you are," we don't know where this manipulation of evolution will take us. Culture is also an unpredictable variable. Culture is not conscious in the way we normally think of consciousness. Culture becomes more or less known by members; cultures can be internally positive (tribalism) and externally hostile (to other tribes). Or cultures can become forces for the common good globally. This takes us to the question of whether evolution is likely to be a positive or negative force for the future.

The potentially good news is that it is our social nature that sets humans apart. We are borne to connect. The big question is which way will it go—connect for the good of humankind, for the destructive, or for the neutral (the latter will by default favor the destructive).

In some ways, evolution—the interaction of genes, culture, and consciousness—is neutral on the big question of "What is our future?" We are pretty sure it tells us that it could go either way—very good or very bad (D. S. Wilson's "evolution could take us where we don't want to go" [2019]). At the end of the day, our own belief is that humankind's evolutionary nature as of today (2020) favors cooperation for goodness, creativity, and the thriving of our civilization. But it needs to be influenced in the right direction. Our book is intended to articulate the argument, degrees of proof, and actions that will help leverage the likelihood that "goodness" will prevail in the future. And for that to happen, education will have to shift from its passive role of, in effect, allowing society to deteriorate, to take up the mantle that social activist George Counts proffered in 1932, *Dare the school build a new social order!* In this book we will not be able to take up Counts's dare in full, but the chapters in Part II do start us down the pathway toward a new social order.

> What actions can education leaders take to leverage the likelihood that goodness will prevail?

THE DRAMATIC TOLL OF RISING INEQUITY

For the last 40 years, we find all over the world *exponentially ever-expanding inequality.* It is so pervasive, so out of control that we can only call it an evolutionary phenomenon—it is built into the system as a self-perpetuating, seemingly inexorable force. In coldhearted systemic thinking, for a moment at least, we won't even dwell on its social injustice. Regardless of one's values, extreme inequity is bad, even fatal for all of us if combined with the other two forces in this chapter.

At the macro level, epidemiologists Wilkinson and Pickett (2019) have produced two detailed empirical analyses over the past decade of how countries are faring economically, socially, and mentally in life. We give you their overall conclusion:

How More Equal Societies Reduce Stress, Restore Sanity and Improve *Everyone's* Well-Being (subtitle of their book, *The Inner Level,* our italics)

The authors developed an "Index of Health and Social Problems" that combines measures of life expectancy, trust, mental illness (including drug and alcohol addiction), obesity, infant mortality, children's math and literacy scores, imprisonment rates, homicide rates, teenage births, and social mobility" (p. 3). Wilkinson and Pickett found that all major "health and social problems are more common in unequal societies" (p. 3). In the so-called developed countries, the United States and the United Kingdom lead the world in "worse" health and social problems *and* in inequality.

Wilkinson and Pickett's (2019) main premise is that we need to understand that all of humanity is sensitive to what they call "a deep psychology of inequality":

> We have evolved to be extremely sensitive to social status. Bigger material differences create bigger social distances between us and add to feelings of superiority and inferiority. As people become more concerned with status they become more out for themselves. (p. x)

In such cases "all of us feel increasingly emotionally unsecure" (see also Arnade's powerful 2019 book called *Dignity*, to which we return in Chapter 6). This partly accounts for what Wilkinson and Pickett call "one of our more surprising findings":

> *Inequality affects the vast majority of the population,* not only the poor minority. Although its severest effects are on those nearest the bottom of the social ladder, the vast majority is also affected to a lesser extent. This means that if well-educated people with good jobs and incomes lived with the same jobs and incomes in a more equal society they would be likely to live a little longer, and less likely to become victims of violence, and their children might do a little better at school and would be less likely to become teenage parents or to develop serious drug problems. (p. 5, italics in original)

Before delving into these issues let's put a placeholder on developing countries—a topic to which we will return in the final chapter. In such countries poverty and inequity are extreme as noted by Gillian (2019), a lawyer who analyzes the legal plight of what she calls the Bop or "Bottom of the pyramid"—the 4 billion of the 7.5 billion population at the bottom—who survive on the equivalent in purchasing power of less than about US $8 a day" (p. 281).

Back to developed countries. As it turns out, conditions are worsening, not due to lack of overall money but rather to extreme, one could say perverse, distribution of resources. As we further examine the wealthier countries, we will spare you chapter and verse. The Economic Policy Institute (2018) provided a recent update on the so-called bottom 1% phenomenon. In the past 30 years the wealth of the top 1% (or whatever percent you want to take) has grown in leaps and bounds (the following figures are from the EPI report). The top 1% has seen its wealth grow by 157% compared to 22% for the bottom 90%. In the same period the bottom 90% saw an annual wage growth of 5% compared to 30 % for the top 1% The top 1% accounts for over 13% of total wages; the top 10% over 39% (obviously leaving 61% for the remaining 90%). Then there is Jane Mayer's (2016) *Dark Money* that takes us through how scores of billionaires acquired their money. Or Richard Florida's (2017) analysis of how the poor are faring increasingly badly in the American city. To take two of Florida's countless demographic findings: "By 2014, 14 million Americans lived in concentrated poverty in extremely poor neighborhoods—the highest figure ever recorded and twice as many as in 2000" (p. 98). And "one in four black Americans lives in a high-poverty neighborhood compared to just one in thirteen whites" (pp. 116–117).

We also see the systemic, hidden ramifications of being poor. Political science professor Eubanks (2017) conducted a detailed examination of how the growing automated social services sector affected the poor. Doing an in-depth study of access to housing resources in Los Angeles and a child welfare agency in Pittsburgh, Eubanks arrived at this main conclusion:

> What I found was stunning. Across the country, poor and working class people are targeted by new tools of digital poverty management and face life-threatening consequences as a result. Automated eligibility systems discourage them from claiming public resources that they need to survive and thrive. (p. 11)

In the end, concludes Eubanks: "automated tools for classifying the poor, left on their own, will produce towering inequalities" (p. 200).

Even when the system appears to work, it doesn't. The culprit? Hidden systemic factors. Linda Nathan (2017) was the principal of the Boston Arts Academy, a secondary school designed and committed to the academic success of poor and minority students. More students did indeed graduate with higher grades. Nathan describes how many graduates failed after they left the school and attended postsecondary institutions because of the absence of "surrounding support." Poor students found themselves confronted with hidden costs or missed deadlines that led to inability to continue. While race was less an issue at the secondary school (which was designed to support these very students), students had different experiences once they got to college. Some direct racism was encountered, but most of all what took its toll was being left on your own as an individual where there was no social support, and where being a minority student was too difficult for individuals to navigate through an impersonal bureaucracy (indeed, an impersonal society).

Lewis and Diamond (2015) found the same phenomenon in their book *Despite the Best Intentions*. Riverview High School is a well-funded school that espouses equity for its diverse population of whites, blacks, and Latinx students. Despite policies to the contrary, Riverview ended up favoring whites and disadvantaging others in both treatment and outcomes. More generally across the United States, the same phenomenon of discrimination follows minority students into higher education. Kirp (2019) in his account, *The College Dropout Scandal,* found that 40% of enrolled students—with minorities showing a higher percentage—fail to graduate from four-year community college programs. Equally disturbing is Tough's (2019) portrayal of those who think that college may be the route to social mobility, only to find that it is a bridge to nowhere.

What Nathan, Lewis, and Diamond, Kirp, and Tough rail against is the false assumption that the individual—in this case students in poverty and minority status, including those who want to move upward—will figure it out. As Nathan puts it:

What all of the talk seems to miss is the importance of putting children's experience front and center. In other words, when the emphasis on grit ends up as a stand-alone pedagogy, the context of a student's life and family circumstances is ignored. (p. 76)

We also find increasingly that young people at all socioeconomic levels (SES) are suffering. The poor suffer for reasons that we have just seen; it turns out, however, that better-off students are also not faring well. Increasing numbers of them find that present-day schooling holds little purpose and meaning for them. Some do get the grades, and others are helped by influential rich parents who buy their way into best universities, but it is clear that this phenomenon is wearing thin. Many of these so-called privileged students end up doing worse in their lives than their parents.

The problem of lack of purpose among youth is documented in detail by Heather Malin, who is director of research at the Stanford University Center on Adolescence. In several studies the best that youth could do in response to the question "What is your purpose at school?" was "to get good grades, go to university and get a good job." Malin (2018) "found no difference in purpose between low-income students and their more affluent peers" (pp. 65–66). In fact, we hypothesize that students who have had some difficulty in life and have overcome it (with or without help) end up having greater drive. In the meantime, the unfortunate conclusion overall is that only about 24% of senior high school students "have identified and are pursuing a purpose for their life" (Malin, p. 1).

No matter what the measure, we can say that the majority of students— some two-thirds or more—find that present schooling is not meaningful. Stress is high and increasing at a rapid pace for students from *all* SES levels. For students these days the modal response to schooling is either *alienation* (if you live in destitute circumstances) or *stress/anxiety* (if you are swept up into the academic rat race). In an odd way these findings indicate a new potential for change because so many young people at all SES levels are deeply dissatisfied and have withdrawn. Our rhetorical question is "Could young people be attracted to a better agenda?"

On a societal scale there is even greater trouble. Growing inequity, frozen social mobility, desperate lives of indignity, hopelessness, and eventually resentment toward just about everyone destroy trust and social cohesion. Democracies fail; societies crumble. There is nothing about this scenario that can end well.

Our question—call it a last-ditch effort—is "Is there another pathway?" Can growing equity, along with excellence, be the solution that benefits everyone? Can we help evolution become smarter than us once more? This other pathway to a better future is more fundamental, more related to evolution's hidden tendencies, and more speculative. *But it can be tested!* If we make equity a "first cause"—alongside meaningful learning, purpose and excellence, and in relation to everyone learning—we have a chance of getting an outcome that is a "win for all."

In short, pay attention and make reversing the deadly path of galloping inequity in favor of excellence for all as priority one. It may be the only chance we have. And it is something that education could become good at.

THE SERIOUS DEFICIENCY OF CURRENT POLICIES

The third factor leading us to a systems perspective relates to policies that could influence the conditions for evolutionary success—such as policies related to income distribution, climate, poverty, jobs, cooperative endeavors, inequity, and schooling itself. There are two domains of policy and action. One is societal and concerns inequity and the economy. The other is educational and centers squarely on the school system.

Political action beyond education is outside the scope of our book, but we would posit that this may be the time where, in the words of poet Seamus Heaney, "The long term tidal wave of justice can rise up, And hope and history can rhyme." On the one side is extreme inequity in wealth; on the other is persistent and stagnant inequity in schools. Relative to the former, money to the rich seems insatiable where currently 1% of the population in the United States possesses 29% of the wealth. If this trend is inevitable, we are heading for mass extinction. A big part of the societal solution will have to be addressed politically, and there are some signs that the combination of action at the top (e.g., the rich being concerned, and politicians being elected to tax and redirect money), and the bottom (political uprising) could turn some of the tide. This extends beyond our book's scope, but here is our point: Education must and can play its part in saving society. This is the role we try to fashion in this book. It will require power and persuasion, but we find in our system work that there are many internal change agents, adults, and students together, who see education as the vehicle where equity, excellence, and well-being can be achieved synergistically. Our solution, as we will see, is our model of "new pedagogies for deep learning" (Fullan, Quinn, & McEachen, 2018).

We have said that nearly all individuals have tendencies to be selfish or cooperative, depending mainly on their circumstances. How they turn out depends on whether the *social conditions* favoring cooperation become established. Let's say this a different way: Whether individuals become self-centered and aggressive to others or self-fulfilling and positively committed to others depends on their upbringing, a term we use broadly to include family and society. We are at the point for reasons well covered in this chapter that humankind is flirting with disaster. We see the possibility of a radical breakthrough arising from the systemic forces that underpin the problems.

The radical change we have in mind won't occur because of some top-down transformational system strategy. But it may happen if the most powerful hitherto hidden systemic forces become more known and enabled to do their magic; and they in turn can be leveraged for continuous transformation of how the global system might work for the benefit of everyone, including the universe. After all, systemic factors have done harm for the past half a century. There is no reason why they could not be turned to our advantage.

Thus, we find that the latent positivity of evolution and "the win for all" potential of increased equity could be the foundations for salvation. This takes us to the policy domain, which in fact is the focus of the remainder of this book. Since 2000, the world of education has increasingly focused on policy solutions for system success. It's not working! In the Western world this shift to deliberate system change can be marked by the first OECD's PISA assessment results reported in 2001 comparing the results of 15-year-olds in literacy, math, and science every three years. Now in its seventh iteration (2019), the assessments involve the 35 OECD member countries and another 35 or so countries that have joined the PISA testing cycle. We are not about to carry out an internal analysis of the scores. Yes, the top performers include Singapore, Japan, Estonia, Finland, Canada, and South Korea. The PISA results are not "the end all and be all," but they provide a useful marker. The head of PISA at OECD, Andreas Schleicher, recently (2018) published a book, *World Class: How to Build a 21st-Century School System*. Schleicher states his main conclusion:

> Over the past decade, there has been virtually no improvement in the learning outcomes of students in the Western world, even though expenditure on schooling rose by almost 20% during this period. (p. 13)

Maybe it was the wrong system policies at work that were the culprits. Our Finnish colleague, Sahlberg (2012), called the problem the spread of bad GERMs (Global Education Reform Movement). Ideas were spreading, but they were not good ones. For Sahlberg they included standardization, focus on core subjects, low-risk ways of reaching goals, corporate management models, and test-based accountability. Hargreaves and Shirley (2009) in *The Fourth Way* made a similar comprehensive critique of the limitations of GERM-like policies evident in what they called "The Third Way."

One of us had written a similar analysis calling the problem "Wrong drivers for whole system reform" (Fullan, 2011). A driver is a policy and a wrong driver is a policy that doesn't work. There were four: punitive accountability, individualism, technology, and ad hoc policies including multiple ever-changing initiatives. We had begun in Ontario in 2003 to focus on what we later called the "right drivers" (see Figure 1.1, Moving Away From the Wrong Drivers).

In the rest of this chapter we will show how these critiques have led us to a transition point in system reform that is still not resolved in 2020. Indeed, this book, which we affectionately call "the devil," is intended to capture the potentially pivotal juncture where we now find ourselves in global system reform in education. To put it another way, current success in Ontario; California; and Victoria, Australia—the three cases we take up later—have been on the right track but have not yet broken through to attack and integrate equity, excellence, and well-being.

Figure 1.1 Moving Away From the Wrong Drivers

Wrong Drivers	Right Drivers
Accountability	Capacity building
Individual teacher and leadership quality	Collaborative work
Technology	Pedagogy
Fragmented strategies	Systemness

Source: Fullan, 2011

Let us trace the early stages of a possible policy shift from "wrong" to "right" drivers.

Fullan (2010) wrote a book called *All Systems Go* in the heady days of Ontario's success that began in 2003. One of the charts contained a list of nine elements of successful reform. In fact, we (Fullan and Gallagher) both were among the architects of the reform in Ontario along with key others including the province's premier, Dalton McGuinty (see Figure 1.2).

We revisit these elements in Chapter 5 when we consider Ontario as part of the macro picture. The nine elements in interactive development formed the basis of a provincewide strategy that involved 4,900 schools, 72 districts, 2 million students, and over 100,000 educators. And it was largely successful: For example, high school graduation rates for the 900 schools moved immediately from a base of 68% to 86% at a steady rate of almost 2% year after year. Other jurisdictions took a strong interest in the "Ontario story" and began to develop their versions, two of which we currently work in: the state of California in the United States, and the state of Victoria, Australia.

The Ontario strategy marked a milestone in large-scale system change. In 2010, it looked like it might represent a breakthrough. Fullan and Joanne Quinn (2016) worked toward this resolution in a book called *Coherence: The Right Drivers in Action.* Many people loved the 2011 "wrong driver" analysis, telling us that we nailed it, but they also said that we did not

Figure 1.2 Elements of Successful Reform

1. A small number of ambitious goals
2. A guiding coalition at the top
3. High standards and expectations
4. Collective capacity building with a focus on instruction
5. Individual capacity building linked to instruction
6. Mobilizing the data as a strategy for improvement
7. Intervention in a nonpunitive manner
8. Being vigilant about "distractors"
9. Being transparent, relentless, and increasingly challenging

Source: Fullan, 2010

go far enough in detailing the "right drivers" in action. Hence, we wrote *Coherence*, which captured the directional solution in four interactive quadrants (see Figure 1.3).

In the book *Coherence,* we adjusted the formulation so that the parallel comparisons were clear: Fragmented strategies became Focus; Individualism became Collaboration; Technology was driven by Pedagogy; and Punitive Accountability became Securing Accountability.

Fullan and Quinn made the case that the four new right drivers in interaction resulted in *coherence.* We concluded that coherence was the solution, which we defined as *the shared depth of understanding of the nature of the work.* The *Coherence* book was and still is enormously popular. In book study after book study, and workshop after workshop, people agreed that "coherence" was the answer. And we had in fact provided numerous examples in the book of coherence in action in named, specific cases. We also furnished *The Taking Action Guide to Building Coherence* that contained 33 protocols (Fullan, Quinn, & Adam, 2016). But then people attempting to use the ideas got stuck. People couldn't achieve coherence by working directly

Figure 1.3   The Coherence Framework

Source: Fullan & Quinn, 2016

on coherence. We thought we had simplified a complex phenomenon; in fact, we called our solution simplexity. The moral of the story is that you can't get complete solutions from a book. You have to work with the ideas in practice, learning the details of success as they apply within the culture of your organizations. It is the interaction of good external ideas and the nuances of local culture that makes the difference.

Remember we are talking in this chapter about three big reasons why we think current conditions could—and it is a mighty big could—result in "system breakthrough" in 2020 and beyond. The first two concern favorable evolution and reduced inequity. The third factor consists of better policies, especially the shift from "wrong to right drivers." More and more people, including politicians, are becoming convinced that the policy drivers that they have favored for the past two decades, including the focus on literacy, testing, narrow accountability, and the like, are indeed wrong—that is, they do not bring about system change. They are not only failing to get us anywhere but are actually propelling us backward.

Excuse an aside here about an intriguing aspect of the phenomenon of change. People find it easier and more compelling *to critique* a situation than *to resolve it.* Fullan (2015) wrote a whole book about this in which he made the distinction between "freedom from" vs. "freedom to" change. The former involves working hard against something you don't like; the latter happens when you get stymied when it comes to the solution, even after getting rid of what you did not like. This also explains a curious reality about task force reports at times of crisis or potential change. When a task force nails the *problem*, it is seen as a brilliant piece of work. Put differently, it is given way more credibility, in fact often revered, than it deserves. Why? Because when you look at the situation closely, you find that the report is much better at identifying what is wrong than in providing solution-related ideas. It typically utterly fails to help get on a pathway to solving the problems themselves. A classic example is *A Nation at Risk* (National Commission on

> More and more people, including politicians, are becoming convinced that the policy drivers they have favored for the past two decades, including the focus on literacy, testing, narrow accountability, and the like, are indeed wrong.

Excellence in Education, 1983), but we could name 30 more over the past three decades.

We are not being overly harsh here as much as we are talking about the nature of the beast. It is comparatively easier to criticize what already exists—we know it and can be specific—compared to coming up with solutions, which by definition are unknown and subject to the dynamics of future actions. And actually implementing those solutions when they are at best partially known presents a whole new level of challenge. Compounding the problem of system improvement has been the tendency to add scores of categorical programs and other ad hoc solutions. In fact, this phenomenon—the unknown solution, piecemeal programs, and failure to implement—is why we need systems thinking in action.

The promising news—our point in this chapter—is that more and more people at all levels are becoming convinced that current policies simply do not work and have not worked over the past two decades. We now at least have Leonard Cohen's "that's how the light gets in." The crack in the status quo is becoming more obvious to more and more people.

The solution we favor and pursue throughout this book entails the mobilization of all three levels of the system (local, middle, and top)—independently and in concert—to focus simultaneously and systemically on equity, excellence, and well-being.

CONCLUSION

The three forces that we have examined in this chapter—the evidence of evolutionary tensions, the dramatic rise of inequity, and the palpable inadequacy of current policy—will result in some upheaval no matter what we do. The world is rapidly and increasingly becoming more troubled to the point that literacy, numeracy, high school graduation, and the like may be important foundational goals but are no longer nearly up to the challenges we face. Our students need these foundational goals; they also need much more. We have already seen that the majority—at least two-thirds—of students are bored, alienated, stressed, or all three. Present-day schooling, and this has been increasingly the case for at least two decades, is painfully unfit for the learning that is required for survival let alone "thrival."

Further, the forces that are wracking society are making their way into school: worsening climate change, ambiguous and scary job market, limited social mobility, tribal-like conflict, deterioration of trust, and the erosion of social cohesion. Within schools there is a growing sense of ill-being, insecurity, futility with respect to the purpose of schooling, and vulnerability among the young. We need a very different school system and one that engages the world as part of a proactive solution. We are pursuing such a solution in partnership with schools in eight countries under the banner of *Deep Learning: Engage the World Change the World* (Fullan, Quinn, & McEachen, 2018; Quinn, McEachen, Fullan, Gardner, & Drummy, 2020). All of us should shift our policy and cultural action toward the equity/excellence/well-being triumvirate.

Artificial intelligence is the machine version of deep learning. We need a human solution, which is what our work strives to develop in partnership with school systems at all levels. The giant shift in the role of schools is not only to prepare students and schools for a troubled world, but to be part of a radically new solution from day one—a goal that we linked earlier to George Counts's 1932 challenge: *Dare the school build a new social order*! The answer is, yes, it should dare, but the proposition is a hell of a lot more complicated some 90 years later.

We need to say as well that *no system in the world* has yet figured out the solution. Anxiety, stress, and ill-being are at all-time highs and continue to affect students at all SES levels. Problems and tensions mount. Even our best examples of seeming success are not all that convincing. The high-ranking Asian countries with their intense pressure on academic achievement seem to be losing ground. Finland probably has the right culture, but its leaders are not satisfied, and they are becoming increasingly challenged by urban and diversity issues. Moreover, the population is small, only 5.5 million, and as Fullan (2016) argued in one blog, people need to "Find your own Finland." In any case, as a planet, we are losing ground and the loss is taking on scary, interdependent, unpredictable characteristics.

Our conclusion in this chapter is not just that we must act. Urgency has never been a sufficient trigger for collective action. Rather we have suggested that there are three powerful forces that represent propitious conditions for radical transformation. We will need additionally a powerful catalyst in the form of a new approach to system reform—one that involves all three levels of the system—and gets at the interactive details within and across levels. And one that tackles head-on the dynamic power of synthesizing equity, excellence, and well-being.

In the meantime, humans, in less than two generations (about 50 years), for the first time in civilization, have been the cause of creating a potentially "uninhabitable earth" (Wallace-Wells, 2019). Now the question is whether we are we capable of reversing this deadly concoction. Fullan (2020a) calls this the battle of the century: catastrophe versus evolutionary nirvana. We need a new integrated set of forces focusing on fundamental change, as we outline in this book. The glue for this new synthesis to occur is system thinking, not leaving it only in the hands of those at the top, although it includes them, but advocating this approach all the way up and down and across the system. We are back to our turtles "all the way down."

2

The Emergence of System Solutions

. . . .

For the simplicity that lies this side of complexity
I would not give a fig, but for the simplicity that lies on the other
side of complexity I would give my life.

—*Oliver Wendell Holmes Jr.*

System dynamics and impact of course occur even if no one is intervening. Some of these consequences will be positive and some negative and they in turn will generate more of their kind. In Chapter 1 we basically concluded that the consequences with respect to the current trajectory could easily be negative, although evolution may surprise us and save the day for another generation or more. Leaving it to random evolution is a big chance to take. For system dynamics to be favorable we need to dramatically increase the proportion of system thinkers and doers at all levels of the system.

In this chapter, and in Part II we hope to show that this abstract, almost fanciful proposition can become a practical reality. The foundational argument is threefold. First, adding more rational strategies to cover complex contingencies has reached its limits. At some point, and that has passed us a while ago, the greater you strive to contend with complexity the more clutter you achieve. Second, we need to find high leverage, and in many ways simple (and we say high-yield) strategies for increasing the participation of players at all three levels of the system. The only system thinking that is consequential is when a lot of people of all ages and levels in the system are doing it. The goal is to populate the planet with people who are tuned into the system and committed to working together to effect positive change. These are the citizens of the future. Third, to accomplish this, we must design our education systems so that each of three levels—local, middle, and macro—have a system mindset within their levels and across the three. An extension of this idea extends to global interactions.

> We must design our education systems so that each of three levels—local, middle, and macro—have a system mindset within their levels and across all three.

We need systems thinking for the following reasons:

1. Rational strategies won't capture complexity.

2. High-yield strategies will increase participation from all players.

3. It will allow us to design our education system to have a system mindset within and across each level (local, middle, and macro).

We know this sounds terribly abstract and ambitious, so you be the judge as we pursue the solution. Such a system cannot be designed from the top down. Yet the solution must cover the whole system. Here is a hint from evolutionary biologist E. O. Wilson: "Neuroscientists . . . are relentlessly bottom up as opposed to top down" (2014, p. 162). Can bottom-up forces help produce a world of natural system thinkers? The counterintuitive answer is that this can be done *indirectly but nonetheless explicitly* by supporting and enabling action at the local level, linked to leadership from the middle and favorable policies at the top. We are not so arrogant to think we have the answer. But we believe we have a productive line of development compared to the alternatives. The rest of the book focuses on our version of what we might call *system change made possible.*

THE LIMITS OF COMPLEXITY

We know a good deal about trying to orchestrate education system change as we have done so from the inside in Ontario, and from the outside in the cases of California and Victoria, Australia. In Chapter 1 we referred to the elements of reform that guided the Ontario system change. In Ontario, beginning in 2003, we put in place a comprehensive number of components, and crucially we tried to maximize learning through vertical and lateral interactions that enabled the system to learn as it went. The idea was to stimulate peer and hierarchical learning and corresponding lessons and refinements as the system moved forward. As we said, we learned a great deal.

Similar methodology—examining successes and failures and deriving lessons for system change—has been used by Schleicher (2018) of the Organisation of Economic Co-operation and Development (OECD) in his book *World Class: How to Build a 21st-Century School System.* Schleicher identifies 14 lessons for "what makes high-performing school system[s] different." The full list is not important for our purposes but includes making education a priority, setting and defining high expectations for all students, recruiting and retaining high-quality teachers, developing capable education leaders, moving from administrative to professional accountability, and so on. Schleicher also identifies 11 elements with respect to "What to do now?" including educating for an uncertain world, preparing 21st century teachers, encouraging innovation inside and outside of schools, and the like.

In a similar vein, Tucker (2019) of NCEE in his book *Leading High-Performance School Systems: Lessons From the World's Best* identified the nine lessons shown in Figure 2.1.

Other authors are beginning to focus on equity, excellence, and whole system change (Ainscow, Chapman & Hadfield, 2020; Harris & Jones, 2020). All this new attention in the domain of system change is encouraging, but we have the sense that the agenda will not be sufficient to mobilize people at all three levels or even at the top for that matter. There is the perennial problem of implementation. Will educators and others be willing and skilled to embrace the new directions? Do they know how and where to begin? And crucially, how does one get widespread articulation of the *meaning and understanding* of the new themes let alone their multivariate interactions? Stated differently, if only people at the top can articulate the strategy (and we doubt if many of them could do so, and there is turnover, etc.), it ain't no *system strategy!*

Figure 2.1   Nine Building Blocks of High-Performance Education Systems

1. Provide strong support to children and their families before students arrive at school.

2. Provide more resources for at-risk students than for others.

3. Develop world-class highly coherent instructional systems.

4. Create clear gateways for students through the system, set to global standards with no dead-ends.

5. Ensure an abundant supply of high-quality teachers.

6. Redesign schools to be places in which teachers will be treated as professionals, with the incentives and support to continuously improve their professional practice and the performance of their students.

7. Create an effective system of career and technical education and training.

8. Create a leadership development system that develops leaders to manage such systems effectively.

9. Institute a governance system that has the authority and legitimacy to develop coherent powerful policies and that is capable of implementing them at scale.

Source: Tucker, 2019

We agree with the value of many of the ideas proffered by the four sets of authors just cited and have pursued several of them ourselves since 2003. But *we have reached the limits of complexity—the capacity to orchestrate multiple overlapping dynamic factors that interact in hidden, unpredictable ways.* We need a very different way "to manage" 21st century complexity.

Business writers Morieux and Tollman (2014) pose the basic question as "how to manage complexity without getting complicated." The authors show that excessive complexity inevitably leads to complicatedness. Customers—as Morieux and Tollman refer to them—these days have many more options, while organizations—and this applies in spades to all levels of the school system—must answer to many different stakeholders (community, special interest groups, regulatory bodies, and on and on). Using a "Complexity Index" that measures structures, procedures, rules, and roles, Morieux and Tollman found that business complexity has multiplied sixfold since 1955 (p. 5). Across a representative sample of companies the authors found that "this index has increased annually by 6.7%, which, over the 55 years we studied yields a 35 fold increase" (p. 6). Further, "over the past 15 years, the number of procedures, vertical layers, interface structures, coordinating bodies, scorecards and decisional approvals has increased dramatically—between 50% and 350% depending on the company" (Morieux & Tollman, 2014, p. 7)

Maximizing rational complexity rests on "the belief that structures, processes, and systems have a direct and predictable effect on performance as long as managers pick the right ones" (p. 10). This means that everyone in the system must behave accordingly, which is clearly an impossibility once you reach a certain level of complexity. Morieux and Tollman conclude that "the real curse is not complexity so much as 'complicatedness'" (p. 5). Our solution—participants at all three levels becoming more aware of the details, more capable, and more oriented to taking action to implement change—is to build into the dynamics of the system the likelihood that desirable emergent solutions will accrue—indirectly but nonetheless explicitly.

As society evolves, as system dynamics become too complicated to control directly, we reach the limits of rational complexity. This is a universal law applied to all social phenomena. Law professor Gillian Hadfield for example, examined in historical detail "why humans invented law and how to reinvent it for a complex economy" (Hadfield, 2019). Hadfield draws the same conclusion we do. For a while increasing complexity can resolve most matters *until society serves up so much dynamic interaction that it can't be understood let alone controlled:*

> [I]nitially a successful complex strategy for solving problems facing a society makes increasing complexity worthwhile. Eventually, however, precisely because the strategy succeeds, it requires more and more complexity to support the more complex society it has fostered. To the extent that the society continues on with the *same strategy* that produced its initial success, the one that already exhausted the easy gains, it eventually hits the limits of complexity and then swiftly unravels. (Hadfield, 2019, p. 168, italics in original)

In law, as well as in any social phenomenon, there comes a point where layering on more complexity grinds the system to a halt. It becomes incomprehensible to the vast majority of system members, impossibly expensive to navigate in terms of time and money, and out of reach for any central agency to *directly control.* Before long, as central players work to get it maximally right, you end up with the opposite to what you want— what we call "striving for complexity and achieving clutter."

We might call the solution to this problem "beyond complexity" or *system change made possible.* It involves system direction, but it also requires other levels to have degrees of autonomy or decentralized authority. The question is how does "the system" have some control when things are decentralized? Well, the system is not decentralized in the sense that people do whatever they please. Some of the controls exist in the incentives that the top provides, especially if these are compatible with local goals. Other controls are "hidden," so to speak, in the motivations and data that are generated by the interaction built into the system within and between levels. In our work and that of others, we have, for example, resolved the tension between autonomy and collaboration. The answer is that *both* are required. Autonomy is not isolation, which is bad for you and for the system. Collaboration is not automatically good: You can collaborate to do bad things or nothing. Rather, people need to cycle back and forth from being autonomous to being in the group—getting and contributing good ideas all the while. We referred to this earlier as "connected autonomy"; others call it "collaborative professionalism" (Hargreaves & O'Connor, 2018; and Datnow & Park, 2019). It works to generate both innovation and its integration into collective efficacy and system improvement. Collaborative professionalism improves the efficacy of the group, but it also carries over to improve individuals when they are on their own.

We can see the relationship between autonomy and collaboration at two levels: between the individual and the group; and between the group, and a larger entity (e.g., school to district; and district to region or state). Relative to the former, for example, Datnow & Park (2019), in their study of high-performing/high-poverty schools, found that teachers were informed by their peers, shared successful practices, and often pursued their own solutions. As the authors put it: "Teachers respected each other's differences, but maintained unity" (p. 69). Similarly, effective collaborative schools maintain a degree of autonomy from their districts; and "positive outlier" districts find their own pathways within the context of state policies (see Burns, Darling-Hammond, & Scott, 2019; and Hargreaves & O'Connor, 2018). We call this phenomenon "connected autonomy." When it comes to successful system change, you have to be, to a certain extent, your own person (or group), while at the same time contribute to and learn from the other entities.

> The art of system change is to help people individually and collectively access and understand how the system operates, so that they can behave differently to stave off bad outcomes and increase good ones.

In the rest of this chapter we lay some of the groundwork for what Oliver Wendell Holmes Jr. sought: *simplicity on the other side of complexity.* Of course there is no real simplicity when it comes to complex system change. We prefer the concept of simplexity—what we call learning to "talk the walk" with each other and to also "walk the talk" about complex matters. In other words, simplexity is when people are motivated and skilled at working together to get good results. As they work together, they become increasingly specific without falling into the trap of prescription. How to establish this commitment, specificity, and capacity at all three levels of the system is the fundamental purpose of our book.

There are two foundational ideas that enable us to get inside our model: One is called *the phenomenology of change* (sorry for the jargon, but it is necessary); the other involves thinking of the system in terms of how the three layers and their interactions—local, middle, and macro—function together. We refer to this as *tri-level reform.*

THE PHENOMENOLOGY OF GOOD SYSTEM CHANGE

In Fullan's first book, *The Meaning of Educational Change* (1982), "phenomenology" was at the heart of the matter. Phenomenology refers to consciousness relative to the objects of experience. Let's call it one's *worldview*. We are going to up the ante because our solution involves increasing consciousness about things that are not so obvious or what we call *nuance* (Fullan, 2019). System dynamics are often hidden. Thus, the art of system change is to help people individually and collectively access and understand how the system operates, so that they can behave differently to stave off bad outcomes and to increase good ones. The goal is to change people's worldview so that it is more sophisticated and capable for surviving and thriving in increasingly complex times. This means that people will have to understand themselves and others better under conditions of complexity. Moreover, such understanding must be dynamic—it will need to change as the world changes locally and globally in its hyperactive nonlinear way.

We are not here to psychoanalyze people at the top or anywhere in the system for that matter, but the solutional direction where we are heading consists of people working hard at increasing their "understanding of their own world views" as well as those of others. It will not be sufficient for leaders to simply *claim* that they understand their own, let alone other, levels of the system. Such leaders in our model will need to *interact* regularly with others across the system to gain such understanding and credibility therein—and to do so in a manner that generates mutual trust. In fact, our goal in this book is to help the entire system at all three levels become heavily populated with leaders (official and otherwise) who have a persistent curiosity about how to improve the system, and a passion for learning together how to move the system forward through cycles of evidence-informed action and attention to impact.

Our proposed solution means that everyone will need to work on examining: (a) their own worldview, (b) the worldview of their peers (i.e., those at the same level as themselves), and (c) those at the other two levels of the system that they do not occupy. Thus, to a certain extent people will need to come to understand the *systems* in which they work. This will become clear in each of the three chapters in Part II and is not as difficult as it sounds. Ongoing, purposeful interaction and reflection with others rapidly increases what we call "knowledge in context" or system knowledge.

It is only through understanding oneself and others that we have a chance of catching complexity in action. We will identify system strategies that make it more likely that this level of dynamic complexity will happen, but they will also include, for example, empathy and compassion on the one hand, and interaction on the other. Empathy involves understanding where others are coming from; compassion is acting on this knowledge. Interaction is essential, otherwise you will not be able to access the world of others, and they will know this—that is, they will be alienated because you don't understand.

> Those with the problem must be fundamentally part of the solution. The theory of change must be built collectively.

If we then accept the idea that system thinking is crucial, and that much of its dynamics are *hidden* we have the beginning of a practical theory of action. Our premise is that for this to work, we have to dramatically increase the level of system thinking and action for those at each of the three levels and their interaction. To learn more about system functioning, you will have to *interact more* with others within your level and across levels. It won't work if only certain leaders become more in the know. A cardinal rule of complex system change is that those with the problem must be fundamentally part of the solution. The theory of change in other words must be built collectively. It must have what Mary Parker Follett called a shared "unity of purpose" (Héon, Davis, Jones-Patulli, & Damart, 2017).

The change agents in our work are found at every level: the 10-year-old student, the teacher, the retired parent, disaffected youth, the recent immigrant, the principal, superintendent, and, yes, the governor or prime minister. Incidentally, Peter Senge and the related experiments of the Waters Foundation identified, and in our own deep learning work, we have found, that young people—children eight years old and younger—take naturally to system thinking (see https://waterscenterst.org, and Quinn, McEachen, Fullan, Garner, & Drummy, 2020).

The key concept involves getting beneath the surface in order to understand what makes something tick. In *Nuance* Fullan called Leonardo da Vinci the "patron saint of nuance." Isaacson (2017) in his wonderful biography pursued the question of how Leonardo became so creative in so many different domains. Leonardo called himself a *disscepolo della sperientia*, which Isaacson translates as "disciple of experience and experiment." Leonardo's self-described modus operandi was "First, I shall experiment before I proceed further, because my intention is to consult experience first and then with reasoning why such experience is bound to operate in such a way" (Isaacson, p. 17). Leonardo was a person of detail but more for leverage than for limits. He represented the epitome of bottom-up detail connected to larger or impressive change.

Leonardo's mind and action set, and our own knowledge of "system change and the devil," lead to a number of compatible insights. System thinkers (remember as young as eight years of age—and babies for that matter) are adept at detecting hidden and complex matters. We do need leaders of all levels and ages to model these system behaviors and to develop similar leadership in others. This will need to become a "movement" of massive proportions if we are to contend with the "beast" we analyzed in Chapter 1 and at the same time to turn the devil's details to our advantage. So far, systems at best have become more complicated, not more enabling of success.

TRANSITION TIME

We do think that we are at an inflection point when it comes to system thinking for education improvement. As we saw in Chapter 1, more and more people at all three levels have come to agree with Pasi Sahlberg's GERM critique and our own "Wrong Drivers" analysis that heavily directed top-down change actually takes us backward.

Less punitively laden, and more flexible policies and strategies are beginning to emerge, such as Schleicher's "world class" proposals,

Tucker's "leading high-performance systems," and the analyses of Harris and Jones, and Ainscow, Chapman, and Hadfield. Policy makers are also getting in on the act. All three systems that we have been involved in over the past decade have made progress at the policy and practical levels. Ontario developed a strong foundation for system change in the period 2003–2018 (see Figure 1.2, Fullan & Rincón-Gallardo, 2015, and the policy publications, *Growing Success K–12, 2010;* and *Growing Success: The Kindergarten Addendum, 2016)*, although a new government since 2018 is reversing much of the funding and enabling culture for the agenda. California made a radical change in 2013 establishing decentralized funding, greater local authority, new standards and assessment, increased funding, and a nonpunitive but explicit reporting measurement and public reporting system organized as an annual "dashboard" (see Furger, Hernandez, & Darling-Hammond, 2019; Fullan, Rincón-Gallardo, & Gallagher, 2019; Nodine, 2019; and O'Day & Smith, 2019). Victoria, Australia, is following similar policies since releasing its foundation document, *Learning Places: Partnering for Better Outcomes* (2015).

All three of these systems have been on the right track, but we call them transitional because they are still in formation and have complex systems that people at the local level are still trying to figure out; indeed, people at the top are still trying to make sense of system change. The big problem remains: how to mobilize people at all three levels. In Chapter 5 we will examine and compare the policies, strategies, and outcomes of the three "whole systems" we have been working with: Ontario, California, and Victoria.

Even frameworks that try to capture the smallest number of core strategies reflect the extreme difficulty of the challenge. Two of the longstanding policy researchers—O'Day and Smith (2019)—recently completed a thorough analysis of the prospects of system success. O'Day and Smith boil the solution down to three major forces: governmental and administrative policy (a focus on equalizing opportunities while avoiding overregulation); developing the education profession (cultivating professional expertise, collaboration, and transparent accountability); and public engagement (engaged citizenry at the community and broader levels). This is a great agenda and we applaud it, but we also know it is currently beyond the reach of most local and state jurisdictions.

As we begin to open up the system possibilities for multilevel participation, let's break into it at the middle level, which will set the stage for Part II, where we examine each of the three levels in turn.

LEADERSHIP FROM THE MIDDLE

We can start to loosen up the system and its top-down tendencies by beginning in the middle, a concept first introduced by the (now defunct) National College of School Leadership in England and developed much further by Hargreaves and Shirley (2018, 2020) at the system level. The general idea is (a) the top can't get it right—that is, the problem is too complex, and (b) bottom-up change doesn't add up—it's too ad hoc and desultory. So where is the glue? Perhaps the answer is that it can be initially found and cultivated in the middle (municipalities, districts, regions, and networks). Neither we nor Hargreaves and Shirley take the notion of working with the middle as the only place to start. It is only a heuristic way of opening up the system question.

Our current rendition of the thinking is presented in Figure 2.2.

Figure 2.2 Flow of System Change

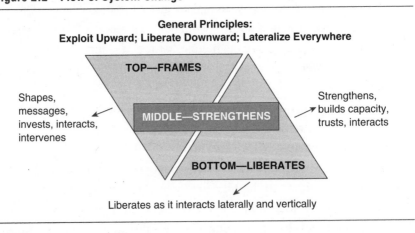

General Principles:
Exploit Upward; Liberate Downward; Lateralize Everywhere

TOP—FRAMES

Shapes, messages, invests, interacts, intervenes

MIDDLE—STRENGTHENS

Strengthens, builds capacity, trusts, interacts

BOTTOM—LIBERATES

Liberates as it interacts laterally and vertically

The model is a bit abstract but we mean it to capture the flow of system change as it "should happen":

1. Starting at the bottom with schools and communities, the first principle is that those at this level should not conceive of their role as

"implementing government policy" but rather as proactively *exploiting* policy relative to local priorities. We mean exploit in the best sense of the word: How do people at the bottom, so to speak, figure out or leverage policy as it relates to their situation? How do they become proactive consumers of policy to the advantage of their students and their learning?

2.   The second principle starting at the top is that in addition to the top framing policy, investing in, and monitoring the direction of the overall system, it establishes the broad intentions for the change, and then it *liberates* those below to do their work. In good old system terms, it liberates people to work in groups where the freedom functions to enable innovation but also serves to assess the worth of what is happening. Peer interaction is always a better form of control than hierarchical requirements.

3.   The third principle is *lateralize learning* everywhere. This is the anti-silo effect. Within every level there needs to be strong and frequent interaction. People learn from each other and about each other. At the top they come to operate as a guiding coalition—for example, giving consistent messaging and achieving greater internal and external coherence. At the middle they learn from each other and in turn develop better and consistent ideas. At the local level, schools learn from each other, and a sense of collective identity develops.

4.   The fourth principle is to maximize *vertical learning* as a two-way street. This again requires interaction across the levels. Leaders at the top need to learn to understand *context* in detail. Such leaders act differently as we found in the 10 cases in *Nuance* (Fullan, 2019). They act like lead learners where they alternately display being an expert (when they have something to offer) and an apprentice (when they have something to learn). They are always learning and always cultivating lead learners in others.

> In order for the system to be effective, education leaders need to interact with the system up and down and sideways.

So this is the nature of the system at its dynamic best. The details are crucial, which is the point of our book: You can't run or be part of the system unless you are interacting with it up and down and sideways as a lead learner. You can't expect the system to develop if you don't set it up in a way where those at all levels have leeway (the freedom from) to act, and the means to learn how to be increasingly present as system players as well as local specialists—the freedom to create a better and lasting future. Crucially, all of this is in the service of the moral imperative of addressing and connecting equity, excellence, and well-being.

CONCLUSION

The concise summary for system change is: Exploit upward, liberate and guide downward, lateralize learning at each level, and form two-way partnerships across the levels. The difference in our approach—the devil is in the details—like that of Hadfield (2019) and Morieux and Tollman (2014)—is that we have concluded that we have reached the limits of trying to corral complexity directly. Rather, the new approach requires a system of interaction that mobilizes and connects people at all three levels.

Context and details therein are crucial. Therefore, any content agenda and strategy will need to uncover and work with the details without getting trapped in the weeds. Leonardo's genius was that he worked in the weeds, so to speak, for a higher purpose—to create magnificent outcomes. In the three chapters of Part II we go inside each of the three levels in order to understand the realities within each level and to look for ways of connecting them to achieve overall system transformation. If details are crucial, how do we access and leverage them for overall system gains?

> We have reached the limits of trying to corral complexity directly.

As we have argued in Chapter 1, in evolutionary terms humans are lucky to have ended up on top so far, but there are dangerous cracks in our future. To stay on top and to make the universe as good as it can be—indeed, to survive—we have to participate as system thinkers and doers. We can't think of anything more exciting—to truly be architects of our own futures. Where else can we find meaning? Who else, other than humans, can help shape their own future?

Now we must get to the details. Inside the details, as Leonardo found, is creativity, infinite possibilities, and the turnkeys to a better and lasting future—but alas, so is the devil. Let's see what these people are up to and how we can help them discover and develop a better future.

Part II
·····································
The Devil Is in the Details

Part II immerses us in the details of the system, according to the three levels of local, middle, and macro.

We deliberately begin with the local level—those traditionally on the receiving end of state or national policy. We then take up the middle level (districts, municipalities, regions), ending with the top (states). Our stance is that all three levels are crucial for success. All are equally important. And when you look closely, all have more or less equal power—especially when it comes to resisting change. Our goal is to refashion the status and understanding of the roles of each level so that those at each level can become proactive and influential agents of change—both independently of each other and cooperatively across the levels.

We realize that each level is complex in its own right and can be sub-divided depending on the system in question, but distinguishing between the three broad levels serves our purpose of getting inside the whole system. Our intent is to provide a conception of the entire system that will give the reader a new appreciation of understanding and working more effectively within their own subsystem and ultimately across systems. Our goal is to help leaders play a role in staving off the further deterioration of society, while creating the conditions for collective creativity and prosperity that humans have already demonstrated historically. The downside and upside potential before us is profound—let's say in the rest of this century, if we have that long!

The psychological frame for each chapter is similar: (1) Endeavor to comprehend your own level and that of your peers at that level; (2) seek to understand the nature of each of the other two levels that are not your own; and (3) gain an appreciation of the system as a whole realizing that whatever level of the system you inhabit, you have power to make things better or worse. The details are within and across each context. The more familiar you get with context, the better you can influence system change for the better.

Underpinning all of this is the assumption that all educators and learners—at whatever level they occupy—must become concerned with improving the whole system. In this sense everyone must become *system players*. When "change forces" are mobilized (in order to reduce inequity, for example) across and between all levels of the system, we have a chance to transform the system; and when the whole system is engaged, improvements are more likely to be sustainable over time even when leadership changes.

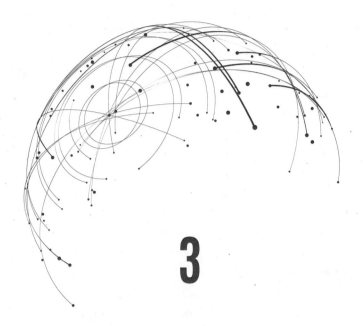

3

The School
The Leading Edge of Change

· ·

s we said earlier, 80% of our best ideas come from "leading practitioners" (or we could have said "lead learners"). This is more than
an ad hoc insight. It tells us that the center of gravity for change may
be more local than central. It is surprising to us then that so little system
change conversation actually begins with a discussion of our students and
their world. Yet when one looks closely at any of the international jurisdictions where systemwide improvement has actually taken place over a
period of time, they are characterized by clarity of vision and goals that
focus on changes in student learning (all the rest are likely to be strategies).

We have shown in Part I that for today's world the goals of education have been too narrow or the bar set too low.

Systems succeeding in improvement respond to the deep moral purpose of building better futures with their children by simultaneously focusing and delivering upon all three areas of equity, excellence, and well-being, and their collective impact on supporting students and future citizens to "become better at life." They do this by reaching higher toward the goals we identify in deep learning and engaging students differently in identifying purpose and passion in leading their own learning. We include in this deep learning very high standards in literacy and numeracy for all students. If our purpose is to improve student learning and well-being, then the start of our discussion must be the student and clarity about the high expectations we know we can set with our students for our classrooms, schools, and the system. Ultimately, success involves transforming "the culture of learning" and related changes in "the culture of equity" (i.e., being attuned to the hidden barriers that privilege some while disadvantaging others). Learning and equity together feed well-being resulting in what we refer to as "becoming good at life" in challenging times.

Our theory of action starts with the observation that each of the three levels—local, middle, and macro—are semi-autonomous. In this chapter we talk about local schools and communities. In the vignettes we present below, none of them *required* policy approval from above. Put another way, local schools can and should exercise initiative with respect to community and system priorities. You can't chisel change from the top. Our book recalibrates the relationships within and across the levels showing how each level can be more powerful than they are today while increasing their influence over each other. A word on terminology: for ease and variety of communication, we use the terms *local* and *bottom* interchangeably, as well as *middle* and *regional*, and *top* and *macro*. None of the levels are homogeneous—local includes students, teachers, parents, community; middle includes districts and regions; and macro consists of politicians, and bureaucrats. There is a case to be made that local should consist of schools *and* their districts. Frankly, we struggled with this but decided to treat schools as local and districts as middle. For some purposes you could analyze the role of schools and districts as the local entity, but this does not change the gist of our argument. Schools and districts need to have degrees of autonomy from each other as well as be engaged in connective action.

Our overall argument is that successful system improvement must be led at every level of the system. System change is dynamic and cultural. It depends on relationships within and across the levels in the system. It is less like a flight plan to travel from one destination to another than it is a loose and flexible formation of travelers moving in the same direction, constantly checking and updating their positions and direction, relying upon each other for updates with respect to course and conditions affecting the journey. Our advice to the reader is to start wherever you are; do not wait for someone else at some other level to get things started or to get it right. Figure 3.1 displays the three systems levels.

Figure 3.1   System Levels

Local	Middle	Macro
bottom	*regional*	*top*
students	districts	politicians
teachers	regions	bureaucrats
parents	municipalities	
community		

In this chapter we start with the local level (Figure 3.2).

Figure 3.2   Local Level

....

LIVING LOCALLY

....

Our point of departure is "living locally." In this book we are going from the ground up. We want to establish the frame that equity, excellence, and well-being must operate as a foundational trio. Then, we will offer eight interrelated strategies for improving local schools and communities—strategies that are within local control of most jurisdictions.

We acknowledge that in authoritarian, repressive, and genocide-driven regimes there are other fundamental problems that must be first confronted and resolved before our book could become helpful. But any democratic country or one on the way to democracy would be well served by turning the system on its head and asking how can the bottom play the role of change agent, and how do we enable such mobilization across the three levels? Recall also that in all democratic countries—as well as elsewhere—inequity is rapidly on the rise—a phenomenon that cannot end well and must be reversed. Some of these local conditions are horrendous. See for example the ACE index (Adverse Child Experience) (Burke Harris, 2018). ACE assesses ten conditions concerning abuse, neglect, and household dysfunction, such as drugs, mental illness, incarceration of a family member, and so forth. Some students show scores of eight or more on the scale and are truly in destitute circumstances that have long-term negative consequences but can be reversed with the right interventions and supports.

The problems, in other words, are massive and deeply rooted, and they are also increasingly pervasive as students of all SES levels encounter anxiety, stress, and substance abuse—all the more reason for the bottom to be part of driving the solution. So, how should we think about the bottom and what can it do for itself?

In the 1970s Weatherly and Lipsky (1977) wrote a breakthrough article titled "Street-level Bureaucrats and Institutional Innovation: Implementing Special Education Reform." In this study of the implementation of new federal special education legislation, the authors found that macro policy could not specify and monitor the details of implementation and that consequently, and de facto, local implementers exercised considerable discretion with respect to whether and how they implemented the policy. The authors placed a fascinating focus on implementation when they concluded: "In a significant sense, the street-level bureaucrats *are the policymakers* in their respective work arenas" (p. 172, italics in original).

In another sense (and recall we are talking about living locally), there are entire bodies of literature describing how students are overloaded (facing the rat race for grades, or the trauma of daily survival), how parents grapple with poverty, educators coping with initiative fatigue (Huberman, 1983, called their plight "recipes for busy kitchens"), and weekly "administrative interruptions" from above. Locals are overloaded, but they can help themselves by focusing on a smaller number of core priorities and addressing them well. They can become proactive consumers of policy without acting like they must do everything that is coming down the pike.

We will take up middle-level and system level roles later, but for now we want to make the point that the lower level will always be bombarded with demands. The solution, as we said in our overall model, is to work on local priorities and to become selective adapters of external policy in relation to these priorities. Datnow and Park (2019) in their study of high poverty schools in California found that successful schools focused on a core of effective practices, while helping to "buffer teachers from external demands" that diverted their attention from key learning goals. These schools also had strong focused collaborative teams that zeroed in on best pedagogy for their students, continuous improvement, and evidence related to impact on student progress. The schools were successful, relative to system learning goals, because they maintained their focus. We will report on similar results in Chapter 4 when it comes to school districts on the move.

> Successful schools focused on a core of effective practices, while helping to "buffer teachers from external demands" that diverted their attention from key goals.

All the better if the policy level (Chapter 5) is going in a direction favored by locals. In this case, the locals can exploit or leverage the direction. If the top is not focusing on the necessary goals to engage students about the future or is serving up a lot of distractors, it is all the more critical that the locals take initiative, that is, be the force of change they want. The top can certainly constrain local choice and action, but the bottom has much more leeway than they realize. The latter, namely, the bottom as a force for change, is exactly what we are finding in our "deep learning" work that we will refer to with examples throughout this book. Our deep learning focus is on the six Cs—character, citizenship, collaboration, communication, creativity, and critical thinking—supported by innovative learning designs and collaborative cultures. The learning work essentially is about "engaging the world to change the world" (see Fullan, Quinn, & McEachen, 2018; Quinn, McEachen, Fullan, Gardner, & Drummy, 2020). We will be returning to this deep learning work from time to time across the chapters.

Still within the local level, if the question is that the local level may not move on its own, there are two responses: One is that our model still has forces for change coming from the middle and the top. Along with this, lateral learning within the local level becomes a powerful force in its own right because the most influential factor in change is peers leading the way.

THE NEW MORAL IMPERATIVE

So, what is the content of the reform, and how do we get there? Our schools and our educational systems need to be "open to learning"—to be places in which everyone is learning and taking action based upon what they have learned. The high-level goals we espouse are *excellence, equity,* and *well-being*, and their connection to *becoming good at life*. We see these four elements as key pieces of the system improvement puzzle that fit together to make the whole picture. You cannot improve a system or a school over the long term without attending to and developing clarity with respect to all four. In fact, we would say that the fate of these forces is intertwined, that is, you cannot get anywhere unless you are focusing on all four and their connections. Each of the four pieces of the "success" wheel is essential and will operate synergistically as you develop and connect them (Figure 3.3). In essence, the four represent the new "moral imperative" of education—replacing the more narrow "raise-the-bar-and-close-the-gap" standard relative to literacy, numeracy, and high school graduation.

In the rest of this section we flesh out the argument focusing on the new moral imperative. We intersperse the text with vignettes that

Figure 3.3   The New Moral Imperative

illustrate the four concepts and their interaction. We believe that Ontario was successful in its pursuit of improved literacy and numeracy learning, and equity therein because its teachers would not simply focus on the lower level and introductory skills. Educators also worked to integrate a powerful focus on equity in foundational skills into and across the broader curriculum, and engaged deeply in collaborative inquiry and knowledge building with their students as stepping-stones to greater student meta-cognition, actually preparing their students to learn for a lifetime. Only a few schools have moved solidly into helping students become connected to life, and the associated deeper learning we espouse, but many were becoming engaged in that direction. Our worldwide work in "new pedagogies for deep learning" has been especially powerful because it has been centered within the local level or bottom—later we will also show how the middle and top enabled some of this work but needs to do much more.

Basically, we hold the conclusion that learning must be deeply engaging and developed in relation to issues that are of prime importance to the learner and to the local and/or global society in which they live. After working with 2,000 or more schools in many countries over the past five years, the theme that has crystalized (created by students as much as by us) is "engage the world change the world" (Fullan, Quinn, & McEachen, 2018).

We start with the rather curious notion of "becoming good at life." We employed the neuroscientist on our team, Jean Clinton, to help:

> People "become" good at life when they feel safe, valued, and have a sense of purpose and meaning. There is a need to be engaged in meaningful activities that contribute to the well-being of others. In the face of adversity, being able to navigate to the resources that you need to get out of the situation—known as resilience—is an essential component. To get there one needs to identify values, goals, and needs as well as personal strengths. The competencies you need to achieve this, I think, are the 6Cs as long as compassion and empathy are emphasized. (Jean Clinton, personal communication)

There are two crucial conditions that must accompany this quest. First, it must be conceived of as both an individual and a collective journey. Thus, the individual and the collective (other people and groups) should aspire to this overarching goal, including pressuring and partnering with each other. One could also say that either one—the individual or the group—should push even if the other party doesn't seem capable or interested.

The second condition, as we have argued, is that *all three* of equity, excellence, and well-being are treated as essential to achieve the moral imperative of becoming good at life. The fates of our four core concepts are intertwined. Let's start with equity returning at the end to "become good at life." Next to climate change, growing and towering inequity is the greatest threat to the survival of humankind. It is at the point where social mobility, through education, for example, has become incredibly difficult except for the lucky few and the persistent. Tough (2019, Chapter IX) documents in detail how social mobility through education was embraced by society and the public in the period of post–World War II and continued favorably for 30 years or so. Sometime in the 1970s and the 1980s things began to change. Rhetoric notwithstanding, mobility became less evident and policy commitments less convincing. Lip service replaced the tough devotion to getting the job done. Shortly after being elected, President

Barack Obama gave a rousing "going to the moon" speech in which he noted that America used to be number one in the world in college graduation, and in 2009 it was 12th. In his first address to Congress in February 2009, Obama stressed that "we need and value the talents of America" and announced:

> That is why we will provide the support necessary for all young Americans to complete college and meet a new goal: By 2020, America will once again have the highest proportion of college graduates in the world. That is the goal we can meet. (quoted in Tough, 2019, p. 321)

By July 2009, this American Graduation Initiative was presented to Congress with a $12 billion investment price tag. On the way to validation, the proposal, in Tough's words, "disintegrated." Well, it is now 2020 and the United States is still in 12th place (or lower). Even more remarkable, says Tough, "is that no one in power seems particularly distressed" (about the failure). We can state it differently. Compared to 1970, American society in 2020 cares less about social mobility! One could say, judged by its actions on the ground, and the results therein, that America and other countries have become less committed to equity than they were in the past.

We are not naïve. We see that those who are currently privileged, purposely or otherwise, favor the status quo. But we also know that Leonard Cohen's "there is a crack, a crack in everything—that's what lets the light get through"—is increasingly applicable to our discussion. Slowly, and possibly with some acceleration, it is dawning on more and more people that extreme inequality is not good for any of us. Whether or not it is evolution kicking in or it is a combination of survival and justice, we believe that the time is right for a major transformation, and that the route to such upheaval is to treat equity, excellence, well-being, and being good at life as a package.

EQUITY

Equity, in brief, is "to provide each according to what they need to survive and succeed." Schools can and should employ improvement strategies in the pursuit of equity, and by this we mean equity of outcome, not only equity of opportunity. The most thorough equity policy we have seen is the one developed and adopted by the Toronto District School Board and its 583 schools (TDSB, 2018). Here is their basic definition:

> **Equity**: Ensures equality of opportunities and outcomes for all by responding fairly and proportionally to the needs of individuals. Equity is not the same as equal treatment because it recognizes a social-cultural power imbalance that unfairly privileges some while oppressing others and therefore focuses on redressing disparity—meeting individual needs to ensure fair access, outcomes, and participation that result in equality, acknowledging historical and present systemic discrimination against identified groups and removing barriers, eliminating discrimination and remedying the impact of past discrimination and current oppression. Equity practices ensure fair, inclusive, and respectful treatment of all people, with consideration of individual and group diversities and intersectionality of multiple social identities, access to privileges and impacts of oppression. Equity honours and accommodates the specific needs of individuals and groups. (TDSB, 2018)

In the context of our book, we underscore the fact that inequity goes deep, and despite efforts to the contrary, it is becoming more and more entrenched in the fabric of global society. There are a myriad of hidden and not-so-hidden barriers, which, as the TDSB policy notes, result in "a socio-cultural power imbalance that unfairly privilege, some while oppressing others, and therefore focuses on redressing disparity" (TDSB, 2018). Such barriers are often overt, but we now know that there are innumerable concealed obstacles that are fatal to progress.

The relationship between equity and excellence is complicated, so we want to foreshadow where we are heading:

1. Society and schools privilege certain groups and individuals in ways that inhibit or enable learning. Such inequity is deeply engrained in culture, and if anything, is worsening.

2. Certain gains have been made in recent years in some schools and districts through what we would call "the learning culture."

Such gains are important but not nearly sufficient for individual or societal success on any scale.

3. Recent developments in "deep learning" theory and methodology indicate that all students benefit but underserved students gain even more.

4. Cultures of inequity persist (privilege prevails) so that this problem must be tackled in its own right.

In this sense, excellence feeds equity.

5. When cultures of learning and cultures of equity are simultaneously addressed, overall success can be had.

In some ways progress is being made in helping underserved students overcome initial barriers. Ontario, for example, has done a remarkable job in reducing the learning gap with respect to immigrants (Fullan & Rincón-Gallardo, 2015). In California, using similar policies and strategies, important gains have been made for underserved minorities documented in a series called "positive outliers"—schools and districts that achieved greater results than would have been expected (Burns, Darling-Hammond, & Scott, 2019). Our sense is that progress is being made because of advances in establishing stronger "learning cultures," that is, cultures that promote high expectations, strong instruction, assessment of progress, and focused collaborative cultures. If we add the power of "deep learning," such cultures generate even greater gains. We are not talking about artificial intelligence (AI). AI is the machine version of deep learning. Also developing with strength is the human version of deep learning. The latter draws on the power of social relationships and of the fantastic recent discoveries of the neuroplasticity of the brain.

In other words, our deep learning draws on the power of humanity. Examples of such deep learning can be found in our four elements of effective learning designs—learning partnerships, pedagogical practices, learning environments, and leveraging digital (Fullan, Quinn & McEachen, 2018)—and in the six keys of neuroscience pathways that Boaler (2019) takes up. The six keys are as follows: learning that strengthens neural pathways, struggling that enhances learning, changing our beliefs to change our brains, using multidimensional pathways that optimize neural connections, employing creativity and flexibility that optimize learning, and connecting with others to enhance neural pathways and learning. In both cases—ours and Boaler's—new results are being obtained for all groups. We cite some of these accomplishments in the course of this chapter. The good news is that if you want to address equity in learning terms, attack it with it with deep learning excellence.

At the same time, we must tackle the much harder issue: "cultures of inequity" (thanks to John Malloy, director [superintendent] of the Toronto District School Board, for some of the ideas in this section). Some of the equity factors are beyond the scope of our book, such as ever-increasing income gaps, employment, poverty, shelter, and community and societal safety. But others are within the purview of the school. Cultures of equity have a number of important characteristics. First and foremost, they understand that most school cultures are inequitable for many historically underserved students, such as black, Latinx, and indigenous students. The use of the word *underserved* is key so that the responsibility to change this reality rests with educators working closely with students and their families. By using terms like *at-risk*, we are focusing more of the responsibility on the student who is negatively impacted by processes, structures, barriers, and bias that privilege white students over racialized students. A culture of equity centers the voices and experiences of those most underserved in all decisions. Further, the dynamic of power and privilege is not ignored; rather these two are acknowledged for what they are, which is the unjust way that people may have more or less access to opportunities based solely on their identities as opposed to expertise, merit, and/or experience. While racialized students are the most obviously underserved, the concept of inequity applies to any category of students who are underserved through no fault of their own (those in poverty being one obvious group).

An instance of how current cultures are biased against certain groups occurs when matters of dispute are being addressed. In such cases, we have to ask the question "who is being served or protected by this decision?" If we analyze the decisions that are made in difficult situations, too often the person who has been harmed by the decision is not at the center of the discussion. Rather, we may favor the experience of the adults in the situation or sometimes students and their families who are usually given greater access and/or influence. The reason that they may have greater access is because they have relationships with those in formal leadership positions or they may have identities that are more associated with privilege or they have shared their displeasure with previous decisions in ways that make leaders uncomfortable. Equity cultures ensure that those most historically marginalized are the priority. Leaders in equity cultures consider all of the issues and perspectives but are not compromised by those with power and privilege when making the appropriate decisions.

The situation in the last paragraph is exactly what Lewis and Diamond (2015) found in their in-depth study of Riverview High School (a pseudonym), a school they describe as the following: "Serving an enviable affluent and diverse district, the school is well-funded, its teachers are well-trained, and many of its students are high achieving." The authors pose the big question: "Why is it that even when all the circumstances seem right, black and Latinx students continue to lag behind their peers?" In Riverview, 90% of whites end up in four-year universities compared to 50% of blacks and Latinx graduates. Lewis and Diamond document deep-seated inequalities occurring daily despite the espoused goals of racial quality. The authors find that "It is . . . in the *daily interaction* [read, culture] among school policy, everyday practice, racial ideology, and structural inequality that contradictions emerge between good intentions, and bad outcomes" (p. xix, italics added). In other words, what happens inside classrooms and school buildings is what counts. Even though the goals of these systems include equity for all, in practice certain groups still are privileged. Lewis and Diamond claim that blatant racism (in Riverview at least) has become less overt and may be even subconscious on the part of many whites, but it is nonetheless (and perhaps all the more) deadly in its consequences for the life chances of those students and families affected.

The challenge is that power and privilege for obvious reasons prefer the status quo (there is other research that shows that if inequity gets too extreme, even the rich suffer; see Wilkinson & Pickett, 2018). Those who have been harmed by oppressive structures fight for equity and are often judged by those with privilege as being unnecessarily angry, inappropriate, or prone to overreaction. So, if we are going to interrupt inequitable realities at the personal level, the school level, and the system level, how might we support or facilitate this? *Leadership is key.*

With respect to leadership, see the intriguing and innovative framework from the Toronto District School Board called "TDSB Equity Leadership Competencies" (TDSB, 2019). Cultures of equity need competent leaders who will assist all staff to engage in this transformative work. Leadership is shared and influence is exerted by many in the school and/or district, not just by those who hold formal leadership positions. This is crucial because the voice and experience of those most harmed or impacted may not be represented by those who hold formal leadership positions. Leadership teams are required to facilitate space for those voices who are most silenced and/or ignored. By focusing on those students who are most underserved, leaders create spaces where educators are assisted to challenge their own biases and to look for patterns in their school's data to uncover any barriers that may exist in schools that impact certain students' success. Cultures of equity are also supported by a school board or district that understand that systemic discrimination exists, such as who gets access to which programs, who is suspended the most, or who is overrepresented in special education programs or programs that do not normally lead to positive outcomes after high school.

Our conclusion then is that schools and school systems must focus simultaneously on improving and integrating cultures of learning and equity. Some students need help to be able to access the opportunities a school provides. All students should be on learning pathways to understanding that learning is relevant to them and their lives, that they have much to contribute, and that they can be successful in learning. Children arrive at school with very different levels of readiness for what lies ahead for them. Every school has some vulnerable students who live in challenging circumstances and others who struggle as well, some schools have more than others, and all of these young people are able to learn if we can create the conditions that support, challenge, and engage them.

We often limit the possibilities by having inappropriate low expectations for children from certain backgrounds. A few years ago, Gallagher was director (superintendent) of an urban district in Ontario. The district included several schools in the city core—schools with high numbers of children living in poverty, high numbers in single-parent families living in public housing, and high numbers of new immigrants and refugees who were new English language learners. The school district had worked diligently to address these challenges. The schools were given additional resources, extra teachers, additional social worker and psychologist time allocations, more library books, more educational assistant time, as well as breakfast and lunch programs in cooperation with the community. Staff for these schools were often specifically chosen for the schools; we placed some of our best principals in these schools—the principals understood that being successful in one of our more challenging schools, as well as some others, was a prerequisite for promotion—and teachers in these schools included some of the experienced and most successful educators. In short, the district did everything it could think of and anything research and evidence suggested might work. And yet the outcomes in terms of student learning stayed the same. Gallagher would visit these schools, often engaging staff in informal conversations about their reflections on teaching their students. As the system became more precise in measuring some facets of student learning, specifically, literacy and numeracy in this instance, Gallagher started to hear a different element to the teacher talk: "We do the best we can do. I love my kids, and I want them to learn to read and write and think well. But home is chaotic, there isn't always enough to eat, they have no books and magazines, no one may have time to read to them, the older ones spend their time helping to look after the younger ones . . . the poor dears, what can we expect?" These teachers were inadvertently aiding and abetting a culture of inequity.

Too often in these schools we love our students and give them lots of support, but we don't give them high aspirations. Without ever realizing it, we lower our expectations of what they can do, and out of concern and kindness we lower our teaching expectations so they can succeed. And at the end of the term or year or school career, we conclude these are wonderful children, but they didn't accomplish as much as the students of advantage in other schools, never realizing that even if they had learned well everything we taught, they would still fall short because we didn't dream big enough dreams with them. What could they accomplish if we challenged them and supported them in the right ways in rising to the challenge?

In situations of persistent lack of success, people can become desensitized to failure. They worry because they know they should. But they are comforted by the "realization" that it is not their fault—it's the system, the culture, the home, or the social conditions of the children. We recall an earlier study in England where the researchers revisited a set of "failing schools" twenty years after the initial study. A few of the schools had improved, but most had not. The big finding: those schools that had not improved had never seen a school like theirs that had succeeded (for a positive example of transformation under horrendous circumstances, see the case of Benjamin Adlard Primary School in England in Fullan, 2019, pp. 33–42).

Equity of outcome is our first element of the system solution, and it starts with high expectations that underserved students can and will succeed. The recent work on collective efficacy is instructive on this count. Collective efficacy consists of a combination of shared beliefs and expectations that "these" students before us will succeed, appropriate high-yield pedagogical strategies that do, in fact, work, evidence that measurable learning is happening, and the presence of school leaders and teachers who work together to make it happen, and engage in continuous learning and further improvement (Donohoo & Klatz, 2020). All of this occurs within what we called above the learning culture, and they do help reduce inequity for some. We also argued strongly above that schools must take the extra step and confront elements of cultures of inequity. This is the only way to make substantial gains in reducing equity across the board.

Equity is not just about graduating or even going to college or university. There are a significant number of our students who graduate from high school thrilled that they don't have to go to school anymore. Most of these young people have no sense of direction going forward with their lives, and even worse, they don't see themselves as capable and creative architects of their own futures. They have no sense of their own power to change their lives and their world.

> Deep learning is good for all students but is especially suited for students who are alienated or otherwise disconnected.

Many of those going to college or university don't fare much better. David Kirp (2019) documents the shocking fact that in the United States four out of 10 students who start college drop out, with figures from Blacks and Latinx being higher. Similarly, Tough (2019) traces in detail how the American system of higher education that set out to be a "powerful engine of mobility" currently "functions as something: closer to the opposite; an obstacle to mobility, an instrument that reinforces a rigid social hierarchy and prevents them from moving beyond the circumstances of their birth" (pp. 19–20). Admittedly, this is not something that can be resolved from the local level, but it is part of the equation where the bottom remains victims of a system where the pressure for reform must come from all three levels. And of course, it shows the culture of inequity that is entrenched in post-secondary institutions.

In the course of our deep learning work, a stunning and powerful hypothesis is clearly emerging, namely that deep learning is good for all students but is especially suited for students who are alienated or otherwise disconnected. The next two vignettes provide cases in point. One school we work with in Australia has discovered that combining equity and excellence in "deep learning" can be powerful in rescuing students who under normal circumstances would be destined for failure. They refer to this phenomenon as "canary children." "Canaries in the mine" furnished the metaphor that early signs of danger can be detected (in this case, canaries whose lungs detect bad air in the mines thereby alerting miners of impending disaster). In schools it is possible to be similarly sensitized and equipped to take action. We present the following in two parts in Vignette 3.1: Part A is the school's thinking about canary children, and Part B is a case example (see also Wells, 2019).

VIGNETTE 3.1
Part A: Canary Children

At the school level, reengaging canary children relies on the extent to which teachers have agency in making pedagogical decisions and the degree to which the school leadership expects, trusts, and supports teachers to challenge the status quo on behalf of their students. In our context this has led to all learning design starting with the student rather than stemming from the curriculum. It involves teachers identifying a canary child and then working with their teaching team to explore ways to do things differently in order to develop learning

(Continued)

(Continued)

that works for the student. This includes manipulating the curriculum, redesigning assessment, and rethinking routines, structures, timetables, and other perceived barriers. An evolving sense of agency has shifted the conversation from "Are we allowed to do this?" to "Why don't we try this?"

Through focusing on our canary children, we have discovered that in most cases the actions we need to take to turn them around center on the learning design. We have discovered that we are able to empower our students within the current curriculum framework by planning learning based on the students' timeframes and interests or on local or global events that spark curiosity and then drawing the curriculum in. Challenging the status quo has resulted in teachers rethinking their role from teaching content to teaching children. Although we follow and assess against our state curriculum, we no longer teach units or themes simply because that is what has always been done. In this sense the canary child has become the catalyst for teacher and student creativity. The goal might be reengaging the student, but the action is to reinvigorate the learning.

What we are also finding is ever increasing levels of student engagement across the school alongside a decrease in behavioral issues. The canary child concept has focused our attention on thinking outside the box while still working firmly within the box in order to make changes at the school level that best impact the experience of school for our learners (Rebecca Wells, interview, 2019).

VIGNETTE 3.1
Part B: Canary Child, Example

Jacob, Age 8 When Intervention Occurred

Jacob's teacher was concerned with his increasing disengagement from his learning, which seemed to coincide with angry outbursts, storming out of class, and disruptive behavior. This was coupled with frequent visits from his brother, who would wander into Jacob's classroom during learning time. The two boys would end up exchanging angry words, often resulting in physical fighting in the corridor. All of this had a significantly negative impact on the students in both children's classes as well as the learning of both boys.

In addition to working closely with Jacob's family to understand what was impacting his behavior and that of his brother, Jacob's teacher focused her efforts on rethinking the learning in order to engage him. Jacob became the canary child through which an upcoming unit of work would be planned. His teacher's goal was to make the learning so compelling that he would prefer being in class to leaving the room or being distracted by his brother.

Jacob's teacher used her knowledge of his strengths and interests to plan the unit. Jacob was social, technologically adept, and enjoyed making things with his hands. He also loved being outdoors and playing games that involved adventure and risk. Together with her teaching team, Jacob's teacher devised a writing project that combined these interests. This included collaboratively writing a "choose your own adventure" story in groups of three or four. The stories were to be published through an online publishing website and purchased for the school library or by parents and families. The real audience provided genuine motivation for Jacob to complete his narrative. In order to develop an understanding of adventure, risk-taking, and decision making, the teachers planned several outdoor excursions. In addition, the students worked in teams to build wooden street libraries (also called little free libraries), which were placed in the local community. This part of the project was designed so that the students would experience doing something for someone other than themselves.

Jacob became engrossed in all aspects of this project. He was naturally drawn to the woodwork and mathematics component of building the street library and took on a leadership role in his group. He also fully engaged in the collaborative narrative writing and was

(Continued)

(Continued)

observed on several occasions ignoring his brother's attempts to distract him. His brother eventually gave up and went back to class.

Jacob completed his narrative, finished his street library construction, and remained on task and in his classroom throughout the 10-week project. His teacher continued to work with his family and other professionals to assist him in managing his anger; however, Jacob's "wins" in class had a significant impact on his sense of self-esteem and on his desire to attend to his learning. Identifying learning that worked for Jacob helped to set him up for success in subsequent units of work throughout that year and into the following year. He is now in Year 4, and although he continues to be frustrated at times, his teachers' growing understanding of the types of tasks that motivate him help them to design learning that maintains his engagement and keeps him participating positively in class (Rebecca Wells, interview, 2019).

A similar example occurred at the high school level involving Gabe (Vignette 3.2). In system terms, innovative examples such as Jacob's and Gabe's do occur, others learn from them, and the system leverages them as examples that are shared laterally and vertically. As we will see in Chapter 4, this is what happens when leadership from the middle becomes a dynamic force.

VIGNETTE 3.2
Gabe, Making Learning Accessible

Gabe is a secondary student in Ontario who usually enrolled in classes that were delivered for the workplace "applied stream." However, he recently joined an academic course in kinesiology because he loved sports and had a strong connection to the teacher, who encouraged him to take the course. Through her participation in a school-based inquiry around deep learning, Gabe's teacher had redesigned many of her learning tasks to allow students more choice on what they learned and how they demonstrated their understanding of the curriculum expectations. Gabe's teacher had her students apply their learning to a real-world context as often as they could. The result was that Gabe, who has learning challenges, could access the curriculum. As an example of such a deep learning task, the students were to explore the nutrition needs of an elite sport of their choosing and create a nutrition supplement from all-natural ingredients that would help athletes prepare and recover from intense competition. During a class marketing forum, students had to promote their nutrition product to industry experts whom they had invited into their class to receive feedback. Community members such as a former professional hockey player, a CrossFit gym owner, a runner who recently completed the Boston Marathon, and a personal trainer for elite swimmers sampled their products and asked students questions about their learning. Through this deep learning task, Gabe surprised himself and his teacher with his commitment to his learning. Gabe was able to apply his learning about important nutrients and calories and connect it to his passion for basketball. When asked, Gabe explained that he was able to learn deeply about this topic because he was asked to learn about something he was passionate about. Gabe reflected that because he was asked to demonstrate his learning in a creative way, through designing a product, he felt more engaged and confident. He said that if he was asked to complete a test, he would have had less interest and not have been able to demonstrate the depth of his learning. Gabe also explained that he was proud of his work and felt like he could learn alongside peers in a way that he had not been able to before (Fullan et al., 2018, pp. 51–52).

Imagine the impact on individuals and society if we could enable success for an additional 20% of students who are currently alienated from learning because of our failure to reach them. We now know that this and more can be done. Initiative at the local level is one place to start. Equity is partly about providing learning opportunities that are relevant, personally meaningful, and supported according to the needs and potential of the student. It is equally about supporting students in exposing and dealing with the hidden barriers, namely, the culture of inequity that stands in the way of them participating in learning. And ultimately it is about removing the barriers. It is about the whole student including his or her well-being as we will take up shortly.

Our argument that excellence feeds equity is reinforced by Boaler's (2019) extensive work on altering pedagogy based on the six keys of the neuroplasticity of the brain that we referred to above: she found, for example, that the students of teachers who took the mathematics course based on the six keys "scored at significantly higher levels on tests than students in other classes" (p. 119). And to our point here: The students "who particularly benefited from the teaching changes and significantly increased their test score performance were girls, language learners, and students from socio-economically disadvantaged homes" (p. 12).

....

EXCELLENCE

....

Excellence for us involves setting and achieving goals beyond the average or expected, both individually and collectively—becoming the best version of yourself. It consists of achieving high standards of performance in particular domains. If our students are to be excited about and committed to the prospect of a lifetime of learning, they need to experience excellence in their formal learning programs and perhaps in their more informal learning as well. Curiosity and the joy of grappling with new ideas can be nurtured. The recent period of improvement focus on literacy and numeracy has taught us a lot about how to improve systems—with each generation of case studies and research, we have understood new components of how to improve. And there is certainly now a growing body of evidence regarding pedagogies (some old and some new), which work more effectively than others. Our focus on literacy, numeracy, and high school graduation has been important, but it is too narrow. In saying this, we are not abandoning the fact that for a student to learn and to think, as well as to share their learning and questions with others, they must have strong literacy and numeracy skills as part of their foundational learning. But these foundations upon which so much else is built are not "stand-alone" skills;

they are tools to be used as students expand their own thinking, challenge other's reasoning, and learn together across a whole range of subjects and disciplines, and this can and should happen at every grade level.

A word here about the claim that "students need to learn the basics well before they can move on to more advanced areas": Put simply, students need to learn the basics as they also learn more deeply in a number of areas of interest to them. In many other areas of learning, we do not expect novices to pedantically work at the basics before we introduce more advanced opportunities to learn. When we introduce children to a sport, they learn basic skills and learn to play the game at the same time. How many young people would have left hockey or soccer or tennis forever if all they did were drills for the first few years and they never had the opportunity to experience how those skills come together in the excitement of the game, as well as how their coach can give them feedback in game situations that allows them to improve? When we introduce children to music or art, scales and technique become refined as they also play or produce songs and pictures, with technical capacity and passion for the product developing together. We rejoice in their creativity as they draw or play, knowing the work will become more sophisticated as their skills improve. We encourage them by recognizing the value of their early work and providing feedback pointing them to greater success and continued creativity in the next product—and they learn to love the learning and the feedback.

Why isn't academic learning just as engaging to our young people? Mehta and Fine (2019) found "in search of deep learning" that they were more likely to find such examples on the periphery, such as in after-school theater clubs, than in the classrooms. We can develop deep learning for all if we put our minds and actions to it (Boaler, 2019; Quinn et al., 2020). Isn't it time to make this the reality for more of our youth? In our work with schools in jurisdictions around the world, we have seen numerous classrooms where students are engaged in deep learning in areas of interest to them. Skilled teachers are able to weave the broad curriculum expectations and more into the daily work of their classrooms. And these classrooms exist at every grade level—kindergarten, middle years, and secondary schools. Our unique point is that they are happening on scale in systems of schools that are creating these ideas together and are developing students as citizens who are engaged in trying to change the world—now and forever. As Boaler (2019) concludes: "It is my firm believe that all students want to learn, and that they only act unmotivated because someone, at some time in their lives, has given them the idea that they cannot be successful" (p. 212).

In our own work we can't help but notice that the best examples of excellence are typically about engaging, understanding, and changing the world for the better. Equity and excellence become seamless. Following are three vignettes that represent "excellence" as students of all kinds engage the world.

VIGNETTE 3.3
Trees Are a Big Deal

On a recent school visit to a group of kindergarten classes for four- and five-year-olds in London, Ontario, Gallagher encountered a large open classroom with a few kindergarten classes and their teachers gathered together. It was an older school in a core area of the city. The school included a diverse enrollment with a number of children new to Canada and new to the English language. The teachers explained their classroom content and their concern about "covering the curriculum" in anticipation of a visit by the assistant deputy minister at the beginning of her visit.

One morning in November our children were coming to school and found city workers cutting down the large beautiful trees that lined the street in front of our school. Our children were very upset and wanted to know why anyone would want to do that. So we put on our snowsuits and marched out as a group to ask the workers why they would do such a thing. They stopped their saws, looked at the large gathering of little faces, and said, "We had a work order from the city." Undaunted, our kids returned to our classrooms wondering what a work order was that it held such power. So we telephoned city hall and invited a manager from public works to come and discuss this and our trees with us as soon as possible. (Who can possibly turn down an earnest five-year-old on the phone?) The day arrived and the city manager explained that the trees had to be cut down because they were sick (Dutch elm disease) and they wanted to prevent the sickness from spreading to other trees. The class was stunned! Who knew trees could get sick? And then in the silence, one small voice said: "My grandma is sick right now; what's going to happen to her?" Soon there were a whole new set of questions, and as they pursued answers to those over time, there were more wonderings, and more, and more. We have now been studying trees for two months, and they still are not ready to move on to something else, except for that group over there who suddenly became fascinated by volcanoes.

As the teachers went on to explain their reasoning, they said first they tried to get the children to move on to another content area, but they kept asking about trees and wanting to gain more information to answer their questions. The classroom was filled with drawings of trees and forests and animals that lived in trees; the children had leaf and seed collections and used acorn shells to learn about mathematical counting and groupings. Finally, about two weeks before the assistant deputy minister's visit, the teachers looked more carefully at the curriculum expectations and realized that within their pursuit of the children's "wonderings," they had effectively included over 80% of the curriculum expectations within the first six months of the school year and had no doubt that they could easily include the rest. As I observed and interacted with these kindergarten students, they peppered me with questions that revealed they had in fact advanced well beyond our "normal" expectations of their age level. It is a rare and joyous experience to have five-year-olds ask if one understood the difference between deciduous and coniferous forests, or why a cactus can grow in the desert and other things can't, and "How do you spell *fumerole?* because they wanted to label their artwork of a volcano. They also explained that a few of their group had only been in Canada for two weeks so were still learning words in English and they advised me to check for understanding when talking with them and give them more time to think through some answers or perhaps allow them to draw their thinking! (Mary Jean Gallagher, school visit, 2015).

Lessons in differentiated learning from the kindergartens! What a privilege. But such phenomena are not confined to the early learning set, as will be described in the next vignette.

VIGNETTE 3.4
Danish Creativity Through Cross-Curricular Interest

One of the graduation requirements for students when they finish their ninth year is that they work together in small groups to complete a major project in an area of interest to them. The project is cross-curricular in nature and represents a major proportion of student time in their final term of school. This particular school had made smaller versions of the same requirement part of the work for students in Grades 7 and 8. Staff reasoned that this provided students the opportunity to get feedback, reflect on their learning with each other and with staff, and ultimately hone their abilities in a number of key areas required for success so they could take their culminating graduation project further.

A group of about six students were gathered working on their Grade 7 project, and they were quite pleased to explain their work to me. They had formulated a hypothesis that fashion and clothing design in any given decade was influenced by the major world events of the preceding decade. They had carefully researched and identified a definitive event for each decade starting with the beginning of the twentieth century. They then identified the fashion and design evidence of a subsequent period of time to see if there were connections that could and should be made—linking World War I and the clothing and dance styles of "the flapper era" for instance, and the space race of the sixties to the invention of polyester fabrics and the leisure suits of the early seventies, and so on. Their intention was to use this information to predict what new design trends might look like given the events of our current time period and then produce a prototype design and dress to share with their classmates. This group of 13-year-olds had a firm grasp of history and social studies and their research skills were evident. They worked well as a group and planned the project and their upcoming presentation together.

Their presentation to their class and parents was going to include a written report, a PowerPoint to illustrate their thinking, and a fashion show in which different members of the group would model clothing (which they had made) from some of the time periods they were studying. When asked about their team approach, they shared that they had chosen their group members based not only on their understanding of their ability to work together but had recruited certain members based on needing their skill set. One student knew how to sew and had made some of her own clothing; another was a good visual artist; one member was adept at technology and would be able to develop their timeline of history and appropriate presentation material. I asked how they knew they would need to consider such things and they talked about their teacher having taught them about research and planning, and group leadership skills, and that also class discussions had included time talking about matching teams to the skill sets needed to complete projects. They looked me straight in the eye and explained that diversity in a team gave better results in thinking! For me, it provided another example of the fact that when students care about the subjects they are studying, they produce and they learn far more than they do when we prescribe the content, and they learn the content we would want them to include as well as some far more important lessons in the process (Mary Jean Gallagher, personal visit, 2012).

A third example is one of many contained in our book *Dive Into Deep Learning* (Quinn et al., 2020, p. 49).

VIGNETTE 3.5
Ask Yourself: So What?

Deep learning isn't just about teaching what is relevant or building skills to prepare for a changing world. It's about reminding the

(Continued)

(Continued)

students of their relevance in the world and how they can make a difference. Teachers who shift to an activator stance have created a habit of asking themselves an important question: "So, what real difference will this make?" In Terri Kirkey's classroom, learners drive their own sense of learning and purpose. Let's take a closer look at how she cultivates this.

Creating an interactive and mutually respectful learning environment is foundational to Terri's work. Terri creates a culture of inquiry by reviewing the purpose and practice of knowledge-building circles. Protocols that reinforce collaboration, growth mindset, and curiosity set the tone for asking questions, wondering, and exploring. This past year, their big question was "How can we use our learning to make a difference?" From the get-go, the message to students is *this learning matters and you matter.*

To feed this question of making a difference, students turn to various resources and partners beyond the teacher. And they are regularly reminded that they, too, bring critical experiences and knowledge to contribute to the classroom dynamic. Terry explains, "Student curiosities, questions, and ideas drove the direction of the learning. We 'shared our brains' and celebrated the experts in our very own room. Students had many opportunities to share their personal knowledge and connections. Students played an active role in the documentation on our Learning Journey Wall. They helped create printable slides to be posted, and students facilitated the connections we made. Students were also involved in the learning goals and assessment by co-creating the success criteria." A strong sense of student ownership pervades the classroom.

Students in this class see themselves as partners in the learning design and also as agents of change. Terry sums it up: As we approached new learning, we often asked the question *So What?* Why are we learning this? Can we connect this new learning to our past learning and/or experiences, and how can it shape our learning for the future? We celebrated connections between what we already knew and what we learned. We began to recognize that these connections help us to deepen learning. We also noticed that it is better to learn collaboratively because we all have contributions to make. Through knowledge building and sharing, we learned that we can teach one another many things and, together, we learn more!

When students see themselves as efficacious, they feel confident about sharing their learning more publicly. Terry explains, "Our learning journey has been shared and celebrated on our classroom blog but also on the school Twitter feed and in the school newsletter. Making our experiences visible to others helps initiate and then expand the conversation for students, their families, and our school community. It also shows that our learning is often linked to our schoolwide commitment to make a difference locally and globally."

It all begins with a simple question: So what?

Students can learn so much from opportunities to go deeper in their learning. Much discussion today in education involves a search for grit and resilience, but just like literacy and numeracy, these are not stand-alone skills or qualities to be pursued in isolation or for their own sake—they are acquired for and through a purpose. Developing educational experiences with our students in which they learn about their own strengths and capacity for learning and accomplishment can allow us to engage them in learning for a lifetime. It can also keep their curiosity and passion for learning alive. Fostering this in a school takes effort and collaboration, but it reduces the effort required to teach for compliance and orderly behavior—ultimately a better education as a result of more effective effort.

WELL-BEING

Equity and excellence buttress well-being, but the latter is more than that. It is about belongingness and sense of purpose about what it means to be alive. Well-being is about knowing, liking, and valuing who you are in yourself, your relationships, and contributions. It is your psychological, emotional, and physical state in relation to purpose, meaning, hope, and sense of belonging. We want students and staff in schools to be well. The increasing numbers of students experiencing anxiety and depression is alarming, and as we have said, no one in any school system in the world has the answer yet. But we do know that some schools are more successful in this regard than others and we can learn from them.

When students are in kindergarten, their excitement about school is palpable. Each day is a new adventure, with time to explore toys and blocks and sand and water and books and stories and a whole lot more. Everyone smiles as they see the students coming through the doors of the school. But as their experience with school expands and they age, student engagement declines. By the time they reach twelfth grade, the vast majority of students are no longer engaged; many attend, if they do attend regularly, out of habit and compliance, based upon the promise of a more successful future if they stay in school longer. The research still supports this promise; better-educated youth have higher lifetime expected earnings, but it is no longer an automatic outcome. Increased numbers of students no longer see education this way, yet they don't see any alternative path to a bright future either.

The answer however could be under our noses. Human beings are hard-wired from birth as social beings, and we love to learn (babies forward). When we are successfully interacting with others around worthwhile tasks, including learning new and interesting skills, we feel better about life and about ourselves. When we visit a school in which learning is open, where students and staff are working together to improve, you can feel the excitement. Student conversation may include sports and social plans for evenings and weekends, but it is also about the projects they are working on and how they connect to the real world. Staff in hallway conversations are sharing their learning and their challenges. If the discussion is about a student who is not doing well, the attitude of the teacher is usually "I haven't found the answer yet" or "She hasn't learned to do this yet." There is a clear sense of efficacy and pride in the work of the students and educators in the building.

Building school success around social, emotional, and academic learning is not new. Research about the social nature of learning has been with us since the 1940s. We now know that much of learning is relational and impacted by relationships and that a safe, supportive learning environment makes a powerful difference. While there is much discussion currently about helping students develop self-regulation, we don't have to reinvent the solution, as McCombs (2004) states:

> When students have choices and are allowed to control major aspects of their learning (such as what topics to pursue, how and when to study, and the outcomes they want to achieve) they are more likely to achieve self-regulation of thinking and learning processes. (p. 26)

We see this personal and collective engagement in learning that benefits the individual and the community (and beyond) time and again in the deep learning work we discussed throughout this chapter. We know that this can be accomplished on a wide scale and that it serves up well-being by synergizing equity and excellence that make a difference for oneself, but also beyond. Well-being involves collaborative and caring cultures, where many people look out for each other. Ultimately well-being involves local and universal identity.

Programs that engage teachers as mentors for students, particularly during the critical times when students can become disconnected as they transition between elementary and secondary school, for example, can make a powerful difference for our students. When excellence, equity, and well-being develop together, they generate a bevy of caring learners of all ages working together.

It turns out that building resilience with our students, enhancing their sense of wellness, is not the outcome of wrapping them in bubble wrap and keeping them safe. It is rather the result of letting them encounter powerful learning relevant to them and connected to the world. It is the result of learning to think, to take risks, to succeed and sometimes to fail, to learn from failure, and to improve. Our own learning as collaborative professionals most successfully follows the same path: think, act, identify impact, learn from the outcome, and repeat. For both staff and students, learning and well-being are enhanced by emotional connections to each other, the school, and the community. In the school (life) of hard knocks, proficiency is an individual and collective matter of experiencing and solving hard problems.

In sum, the totality of integrating equity, excellence, and well-being is to feed what it means to be good at life. The active brain is telling us that equity and excellence are close cousins. This is the new moral imperative for schools in 2020 and beyond.

HOW DOES A SCHOOL IMPROVE IN THESE WAYS?

One of the most important things to remember as a school leader interested in moving your school in this direction is that it doesn't happen in one big revolutionary change—it happens in an infinite number of small steps. It changes through a number of task-oriented steps and adjustments but is largely a culture shift within the school. Culture shifts are about people and how they move their own beliefs and actions. Our best advice is to think of this as a challenge of mobilizing and developing with your staff around purposeful action focused on improving teaching and learning in your school in the immediate future and over the long term. We have detailed these processes in other publications: *Coherence: The Right Drivers in Action for Schools, Districts, and Systems* (Fullan & Quinn, 2016), *Deep Learning: Engage the World Change the World* (Fullan et al., 2018), *Dive Into Deep Learning: Tools for Engagement* (Quinn et al., 2020), *Nuance* (2019), and *Leading in a Culture of Change*, 2nd ed. (Fullan, 2020). For now we just offer a few pointers.

The eight guidelines for school improvement are listed in Figure 3.4. Assume that the content of this work is "the new moral imperative" that integrates equity, excellence, and well-being for all.

Readers familiar with school improvement planning processes will recognize that these eight guidelines actually outline a typical school improvement planning cycle. We include them here because they are key to building a culture change in the school. The difference between these steps being a successful vehicle for positive change in a school and being a time-wasting process of compliance with a district or state's requirements is indeed in the details. We ask the reader to examine these steps with a mindset of how they can be used as staff, student, and community engagement tools. Changing a school's culture in lasting ways—the cultures of learning and equity that we talked about—is all about engaging the people

Figure 3.4   Guidelines for School Improvement

Set the Direction

1. Jointly (with staff, students, parents, and community) develop a vision of the goals and means of learning.

2. Engage a core group in completing a school self-assessment.

3. Develop a set of strategic goals for improved learning for the year.

Define the Path Forward

4. Identify a set of targeted, evidence-based strategies and resources to move from goals to action in classrooms across the school.

5. Continually build the professional capital of staff, students, and community—that is, the individual and collective capacity to learn and consolidate.

Do the Work

6. Implement and monitor.

7. Pursue culture-based accountability and evaluation.

8. Feed and be fed by the system.

in the school in learning their way forward together. They have to own the changes—right from developing a consensus on what the students need, to struggling together to identify what changes in pedagogy will be required, and to what needs to be done to unseat privilege. Fundamentally what is required is a very different kind of learning than what exists in most schools today.

Steps 1, 2, and 3 set the direction and establish the change leadership team to carry the change forward. Engaging the entire school in gaining clarity and understanding of the work ahead and its importance will provide the impetus needed to carry the work through the challenges ahead. Your goals should express with precision what will change in student learning as a result of your work. Important recent developments have stressed that parents, community members, and trustees must be central to local development from the outset (O'Day & Smith, 2019, Chapter 7; Campbell & Fullan, 2019). As collaboration around the development of goals is taking place, staff is learning to work together differently in their thinking about students and what needs to happen in their classrooms in order to build these skills. Professional conversations are beginning to change. Principals with good change leadership skills will notice these changes, communicate about them, and celebrate them, talking about them as the beginning of the new culture.

Steps 4 and 5 (evidence and professional capital) define the path forward, including identifying what needs to be learned in order to succeed. Collaborative structures are being put into place within which that learning will be able to be nurtured. Once again details and precision matter. Be mindful of the purposes: to have the change in teaching actually take place in classrooms throughout the school (the task); to engage as many staff as possible in developing what the change will look like in their grade level, department, or personal classroom (the ownership of the task); and to begin to shift the culture of the school to one that is more "open to learning" (the long-term change leadership and stance that are needed).

At this stage staff might be asking themselves:

- What would a specific goal with impact for the next unit of work look like in the primary grades? In the junior years? In the math department? And so forth.

- What pedagogies would work to develop that learning?

- What learning and equity goals would be appropriate day to day?

- How do we combine equity and excellence for all?

- How is the learning contributing to well-being and becoming "good at life"?

- What learning activities would assist students in strengthening their skills in these areas?

- What timeline will we set for ourselves to implement these changes in our teaching?

Grade level or subject teams of teachers become a consulting and development group together, exchanging ideas and evidence around new pedagogy, sharing successes and challenges, keeping each other on course, and making the work of learning to improve one's teaching a bit more manageable.

The biggest resource needed to support changes in schools is time. Teachers need time to meet, to learn, and to plan together, and this time is in chronically short supply. Creative school leaders, however, can find ways to address this need both during the timetabling exercise and during the year itself. Some meeting time can be regularly scheduled into the timetable to allow teachers to plan and to learn together. Specific learning programs for students can contribute additional meeting time. We have seen some schools use school assembly times to provide time for some teachers to do grade-level activity planning together while the rest of the staff participates in the assembly or large school activities with the students. Other schools have instituted "reading buddy" activities between primary and junior classes to allow staff to take turns working with combined classes so that other staff can have additional planning time. However, if this is all you do, you will not see full results! In deep learning schools, the use of time is radically reconfigured around the pursuit of the 6Cs (Quinn et al., 2019, Chapter 8, "Deep Learning Design").

The final three steps (6, 7, and 8) detail doing the work you have been planning. In these implementation meetings, it would be expected that staff would commit to a change in their practice in their classrooms— implementing the strategy that they have decided to pursue. This is the point at which internal accountability is enabled. Staff commit to each other what they will change and what they expect their students will be able to do in response to the new approach within the specified time cycle. They set learning goals aligned with the curriculum expectations and the larger school improvement priorities. They work in teams in pursuing selected direction and goals. They identify together the things they will look for in order to assess successful student learning. They make plans to walk through and visit each other's classrooms and provide observations to each other. They share representative student work from their classes. They work with students and parents/community as partners in learning. Halfway through the cycle, they come together again to share their observations, their successes, their challenges and to co-develop solutions. At the end of the cycle, they assess their impact again and plan refinements to be included in their next cycle of work.

We have found that the best foundation for evaluation is what we call "culture-based accountability" (Fullan, 2019). This means that transparency, specificity, and nonjudgmentalism become part and parcel of the culture of the organization, which in effect becomes a culture of individual and collective responsibility. This is what Elmore (2004) had in mind when he referred to the critical importance of "internal accountability." What is especially noteworthy here is that the qualities of effective collaboration—focus, specificity, transparency, use of data, know thy impact—are equally the qualities of strong accountability.

Collaboration must also extend beyond the individual school to the system. We believe schools everywhere can become powerful change agents, first for their own student and staff learning, and next as examples and colleagues and mentors of "next promising practices in learning" for the schools around them. By exploiting the aspirations and resources made available by their districts and departments of education—taking every advantage of the resources, training, processes, and funding being made available to them to push their own performance forward—schools and groupings of schools can lead the way for the system.

> Good work and effective assessment become *one and the same.*

More than this: As you spread your semiautonomous wings, you need to learn from others outside the local area: other schools and districts, regional hubs, state-level entities and so on. This is the part where you "go outside to get better inside." You get significant new ideas, form coalitions, and in so doing gain professional and political allies. If you are faced with a regime that has the "wrong" policies and actions, you minimize contact with that level as much as possible, or you join coalitions that seek new and better policies.

CONCLUSION

In our recent deep learning work, as a more action-oriented way of getting started into system change, we have formulated the strategy as follows:

1. Position equity and excellence as the goal and outcome.

2. Base the action theory on the integration of *deep learning, engagement, and well-being.*

3. Relate items (1) and (2) to "life circumstances" as both cause and effect; that is, life circumstances can enable greater learning,

or inhibit it, and better life circumstances can be an outcome or product of better learning, engagement, and well-being.

4. The end result is that equity, excellence, learning, engagement, and well-being as a syndrome improve life circumstances for the betterment of the individual and humanity.

These are the aspirations of the new system change in action for 2020 and beyond.

Most of the proactive work at the local level we have been describing in this chapter is a *system phenomenon*. Thus, locals are just as much part of the system as those from any level. They become more powerful when they learn laterally from other local entities; they become proactive consumers of state policy; they develop as better partners upward; and they evolve as a force for system change itself. System change is too critical to be left to the vagaries of those at the top.

In sum, as part and parcel of living locally with more initiative, gaining ideas and power from inside and outside the school, you need equally to see yourself as a *system player.* If your system is not supporting you yet in these changes, all the more reason for you to engage with the system to bring it onside. You are just as much a part of the system as the president or whomever. This is what Margaret Mead meant when she said, "Never doubt that a small group of thoughtful [organized], committed citizens can change the world; indeed that is the only thing that ever has." Such proactivity is crucial at the present time when there appears to be a "crack in the system" that is letting in the light to new policies that are less punitive and more amenable to new capacity building. If there ever was a time to be a system player, it is now. Interact with local peers, and build two-way multiple streets wherever possible with the middle and the top.

By redefining equity as doable, as every bit as crucial as excellence (indeed as equity and excellence fueling each other), as linked with better learning, engagement, and well-being, and as achievable at the local level, we have the potential of treating schools and communities as autonomous sources of pushing for system reform. The best defense is almost always a good offense. All the better if the middle and top become involved as serious partners, but the main point now is that the street-level bureaucrats can and must be proactive and powerful agents of change. Once mobilized, the bottom represents the most powerful agent of change in the system.

4

The Middle

Fuel and Glue

· ·

O ur tongue-in-cheek image of the middle is that the top tells it what to do, the middle does it, and the locals complain that they are doing it. The middle is districts, regions, municipalities, networks of schools, and so on. When Andy Hargreaves, Denis Shirley, and others noticed that in Ontario the middle (districts) can be quite influential and innovative, it opened a whole new line of thinking. It was no accident that "leadership from the middle" started in Ontario because midway through its reform (2008), the center recognized the limits of leading from the top and established targeted resources for districts as a group to lead the reform, including in special education. Our team has since established an approach that stresses leadership from the middle (LftM), whatever the system.

LftM is only a notion, so the details are critical. It consists of direction, goals, and resources from the center (government), leeway at the middle to work with locals, and the kind of local-connected autonomy that we just saw in Chapter 3. When we first mentioned LftM to various groups around the globe, people in the middle were immediately appreciative. They recognized the empowerment possibilities of playing a key leadership and linking role in system transformation.

Systemwide change may be initiated with goals and planning frameworks from the top, but if impact on student learning is going to take place, it requires "leadership from the middle." There are several reasons for this, as we summarize in the following box.

The Importance of the Middle

1. Government and central agencies cannot directly interact with large numbers of schools at the level of precision required to accelerate and deepen learning. Inevitably, in attempting precision, governments become or will be interpreted as becoming too prescriptive. Trying to build teacher capacity, better pedagogy, and continuous improvement through prescription is a mug's game. Such an approach from the center automatically undercuts the likelihood that changes in the culture in schools will follow.

2. As the first level of system work takes place and early progress is made, moving all schools forward requires increased differentiation of approach and support. The dialogue between a supporting agency and the schools needs to be continuous, becoming increasingly focused on teaching, learning, and observable impact. Agencies in the middle (districts and other regional entities) need to learn their way forward together within the context of the district's and school's culture. Central government (states, provinces, countries) entities are not structured to be able to do this, but a more regional agency or school district body could be.

3. Both the government and its central agencies on one side, and schools on the other, need the advice, support, interpretation, and provocation of a "knowledgeable other" or "others" (consultants, other districts, and the like) who can act as advisors. Many times these resources are found in the middle. People in the middle must have a deep understanding of the system (both the government and school parts) in order to build progress together around common goals and can become a critical catalyst for both local and system levels.

In this chapter we turn to the middle as the key player (see Figure 4.1). Following our respect for the subjective world of each level, we take the position in this chapter that the middle should first strive to understand locals—empathetically—and then understand the priorities of those at the top (usually the people you report to) in relation to how likely the agendas of the top and bottom could connect. It is your job in the middle to help make that link. There are huge variations in what the middle is facing so we don't generalize on a specific model, but we can say that wherever you are, try to first understand what is below and above you. In short, read Chapters 3 and 5 as part and parcel of determining your own role.

Figure 4.1   The Middle

WHO IS "THE MIDDLE"?

In our work with school systems in improving student learning, we have seen different structures, responsibilities, and authority attached to these regional organizations in "the middle." The structures are reflective of the history and culture that have grown over time in the development of education in the state, province, or region. It is not the "structure" of the middle organization that matters to long-term improvement as much as the role and the relationships—upward with the central department, laterally with other "middle" districts or regions, and downward with the schools.

The middle organizations are the regional entities in the education system. In some jurisdictions, such as Victoria, Australia, they are a regional presence of the Department of Education and Training. In others, such as California, they may be regional county entities or local independent school districts. California is more complicated because it has two layers at the middle: 58 counties (that historically have mainly a program compliance relationship to districts—a role that is now changing as we will take up in Chapter 5) and 1,009 local school districts (a few very large districts, such as San Francisco and Los Angeles, are entities unto themselves). In Sweden and Denmark, the middle consists of local municipalities. New Zealand, with 2,500 schools in total, is organized around a combination of individual school councils, and in more and more cases, "communities of learners" consisting of networks of schools working together, typically five or more schools. New Zealand is currently considering an overhaul of its system by creating regional education hubs consisting of approximately 125 schools each, but no decisions have been made.

In Ontario and other Canadian provinces, the middle consists of school districts, created by government legislation and accountable to a locally elected school board. In all of these cases, these middle-level groups began as operational entities, ensuring governance, greater administrative consistency, and easier accountability across groupings of schools in geographic areas. Over the past few decades, these same agencies may have also provided school staff training in curriculum, pedagogy, and leadership to schools. But these training programs were often "one-off" events, designed to familiarize staff with new curriculum documents or other resources, legal requirements, or other expectations—in short, the agenda of the top was "delivered" via documents and related sessions. More recently, as these groups learned more about system change and benefited from the research about effective capacity, efforts in staff development changed as well. Rarely have these staff training efforts resulted in systemic and sustainable improvement in student outcomes. However, the chances of success climb dramatically when these efforts are (1) combined with work taken on by schools, (2) supported by programs and investments from the center, (3) embedded in schools, and (4) responsive to school need.

One can easily find examples of significant improvement in individual schools, and as one examines these ad hoc successes, there are powerful lessons to be learned about developing a school team with a continuous improvement focus and culture (as we have seen in Chapter 3). But all too often these schools would be isolated examples and on their own could not sustain successful improvement over time or as leadership changed.

For districts, or regional entities, case studies of successful districts identify the characteristics of districts that were able to work with groupings of schools to improve student learning. In fact, as research into school improvement strategies unfolds, these districts provide important lessons illuminating the pathway forward. Essentially, these regional structures can provide the "glue" that brings schools and government departments together in the reform effort, to function as a system. As we argue in this book, the limits of holding the system together with top-down resources, even if they are good, have been reached, as systems have become more complicated. We are now, in a word, "beyond complexity" and will need to find more sophisticated methods to stimulate and guide system improvement.

A state department or ministry of education has, if it has launched and supported the reforms, set goals and created a number of tools and resources to support schools in improving classroom practice. They have, no doubt, provided staff development resources as well. But deep, successful system change requires a cultural change in classrooms and in schools. Districts and regional offices have been working with schools "operationally" for years, but not "instructionally." As they step into their roles in leading instructional change, they are potentially well positioned to make a positive difference: They are closer to the schools, they know the personnel involved better, and they know the environment and context within which the schools operate. These regional entities are also positioned close to the central departments of education in states or provinces. They are more likely to understand the larger system goals, processes, programs, and resources. And so they become an important bridge connecting the two levels of the system.

Districts or regional offices can support and assure the implementation of the needed changes at the front line, both through their own action and through their ability to inform and influence both the center and the schools as the reforms develop. They can provide timely research and promising practices from elsewhere to schools when they are thinking through solutions to their challenges. They provide critical analysis "from the schools" upward to the central offices in order to help shape the supports and investments a department may be developing. Most importantly, they provide provocative questions and ideas upward, across and downward in the system as an interrupter of "group think" when teams are working together.

SUCCESSFUL DISTRICTS: STILL IN THE MINORITY

We have worked with successful districts in Canada, the United States, and elsewhere since 1990. Some were successful under regimes of wrong driver policies at the government level: York Region and the Ottawa Catholic School Board in Ontario in the late 1990s; several in California in the early 2000s: Garden Grove, Long Beach, Sanger, and Whittier High School Unified; and large urban local authorities in England: Tower Hamlets and Hackney (for the latter two see Fullan & Boyle, 2016).

> The flaw was that many districts suddenly realized that they did not have the capacity to take advantage of the newfound freedom.

Recently there is a new wave of district improvement under conditions of "right policy" contexts such as our work in California. In 2013, California governor Jerry Brown introduced a radical new system policy under the banner of Local Control Funding Formula (LCFF) that decentralized resources and some authority to local districts in the context of less intrusive accountability from the top. Tom Torlakson, the California state superintendent of public instruction, referred to the new policy as "strengthening the role of the middle" and seeking the "right drivers" for reform. Our team conducted an assessment of the California initiative covering the first five years of the reform (Fullan & Rincón-Gallardo, 2017). We concluded that the policy and direction were on the right track but had a fatal flaw. The policy assumed that if given the opportunity and resource support, local districts would flourish. The flaw was that many districts suddenly realized that they did not have the capacity to take advantage of the new-found freedom—that is, the freedom deriving from the LCFF legislation in 2014, which gave greater resources and autonomy to local districts (see Chapter 5). In previous top-down regimes, most districts had not learned how to lead their own district reforms as they operated more on the receiving end of policies. Only a few were prepared to take advantage of the new opportunities made possible by LCFF.

On the other hand, some districts are moving forward. The Learning Policy Institute (LPI) at Stanford recently completed a study of how the districts are faring under the new policy set. In a quantitative analysis LPI found that in districts with more than 2,000 students (this was the cutoff point given that there were many tiny districts), 156 out of 435 of them were doing better than expected in serving minority students (Podolosky, Darling-Hammond, Doss, & Reardon, 2019). More revealing is LPI's case study of seven "positive outlier" California districts that are, so to speak, beating the odds. These districts represent a new crop of districts beyond Garden Grove, Whittier, and others who are taking advantage of the "leadership from the middle" opportunities, although two of the districts—Long Beach and Sanger—are from the earlier list as well. The nature of the newly successful districts is well worth examining. Burns, Darling-Hammond, and Scott (2019) provide a synopsis of how these seven districts "are pursuing equitable access to deeper learning." These researchers found nine characteristics in common relative to these front-runners:

Commonalities of Positive Outlier Districts

1. A widely shared, well-enacted vision that prioritizes learning for every child.

2. Instructionally engaged learners.

(Continued)

(Continued)

3. Strategies for hiring and retaining a strong, stable educator workforce.

4. Collaborative professional learning that builds collective instructional capacity.

5. A deliberate developmental approach to instructional change.

6. Curriculum, instruction, and assessment focused on deeper learning for students and adults.

7. Use of evidence to inform teaching and learning in a process of continuous improvement.

8. Systemic supports for students' academic, social, and emotional needs.

9. Engagement of families and communities. (Burns et al., 2019, pp. 1–2)

What is most noteworthy in these districts is that the students are consistently outperforming (on state measures of achievement—see our Chapter 5) students of similar racial and ethnic backgrounds (Burns et al., 2019). In a sense we are seeing the district face of the successful high-poverty schools that we cited in Chapter 3 from Amanda Datnow's research on individual schools. All of this is encouraging and we want to mark the accomplishment by underscoring that in California this early success is a function of schools, districts, and the state working together (see Chapter 5 when we examine the California case as a whole). We are cautiously optimistic because we know what it takes to be this successful. It takes tremendous sustained effort of doing the right things over long periods of time. Are these "positive outliers" harbingers of overall system transformation or are they reflections of the heroic efforts of early pioneers? We think it is a bit of both. The key question is whether the efforts in 2019 differ from those in 2000 when we also had a small number of districts that were extraordinarily successful.

Our answer is a strong "maybe." California's current early success is a function of certain districts wanting to take advantage of the new possibilities, along with a favorable framework of support across the three levels. Success in the outlier districts may require such extraordinary effort over several years that it may not be sustainable in those districts let alone in others who wish to emulate them. Here is our positive proposition: If the conditions for success can be made more normal; if the individual capacities in the above list of nine necessary factors become more established, thereby feeding on each other having a multiplicative effect (capacity begets capacity); and if the system deliberately learns from its successes within and across each level, thereby making success more doable on a wide basis—then we may see sustainable system transformation. In a phrase, the possibilities of success are getting closer.

MORE SYSTEM CHANGE

All of this is encouraging and points the way forward. But, only a small proportion of the system is really on the move. We are beginning to understand in what way and how individual districts, municipalities, and regions can become successful. It requires great leadership, rapport, trust, and honesty between school and district officials. Progress involves focused collaborative work that increases capacity and its link to better student learning outcomes—and five or six years of building momentum and getting results. One example of such systemwide district development is presented in Vignette 4.1 involving Ottawa Catholic School Board (OCSB) in Ottawa. This case is especially instructive because it applies to the whole district and involves fundamental change in culture focusing on deep learning (DL). The district successfully introduced Deep Learning in all of its 83 schools (in Year One, seven schools began implementing the program; in Year Two, eight more schools began adopting it; and in Year Three, all 83 schools were immersed in deep learning).

VIGNETTE 4.1
Ottawa Catholic School Board (OCSB)

Walk into schools and you see students working with their own personal devices and using space purposefully for collaborating or moving. They may be using green walls scattered throughout the building to create videos so that they can add backgrounds and audio later. Walls are covered with colorful student-made products and art. There is a buzz of engagement, and students taking responsibility for their learning is the norm.

But it's not just the students who are learning in new ways. Teaching and learning are highly visible with teachers meeting in teams by grade or cross panel to plan learning activities or examine the depth of student learning and work. Teacher learning isn't restricted to planning, because you will see schools where teachers are learning alongside or directly from students as they explore ideas, new digital devices, or resources that are not familiar to the teachers.

Principal and district leaders are also visible learners because they attend student-led workshops or tutoring sessions to learn how to "leverage the digital" medium (one of the key components of the pedagogical model to enhance their own learning or pedagogical practice). There is regular participation in learning walks, where teams of teachers, leaders, and sometimes students visit classrooms with an observational purpose, sharpening skills or both observing classroom practice and providing feedback to deepen student learning. At the same time, monthly meetings of all principals and district leaders are opportunities to focus on sharing and developing solutions to problems of practice.

Making this kind of learning the norm for all schools and classrooms doesn't happen by chance. District leaders describe the strategies and conditions that are contributing to their journey.

Leadership and Governance—Setting the Stage

Innovation and well-being were already at the heart of change in the Ottawa district. Beginning in 2010, a collaboratively created blueprint for change focused on a cultural shift across the board while the creation of a digital ecosystem focused more on staff and student collaboration, creativity, critical thinking, and communication. Simultaneously, the district improved infrastructure, including wi-fi in all schools, facilitated the conversion of school libraries to learning commons, provided laptops for all educators, and integrated software and hardware supports. Governance issues were integrated with the creation of a social media policy as well as the first plan in the province to integrate yearly instruction on digital citizenship into the curriculum. Leaders were intentional in building on these foundations to strategically craft a coherent plan for whole change over three years (2014–2017) and to divert funds to directly support this new direction. It is important to note that the strong implementation was achieved without new money but by focusing direction and realigning district priorities, programs, and digital practices to support it.

Whole System Mindset

The senior leadership team of the district recognized that NPDL (New Pedagogies for Deep Learning) was aligned with the board's focus on pedagogy as a driver and leveraging technology to create new learning and teaching opportunities. Strategically, the first set of seven schools were identified to participate in NPDL. Schools were selected based on one per academic superintendent's family of schools to ensure that all superintendents were part of the leadership process along with a school in each trustee's zone. Each superintendent selected a school that had a supportive principal and a staff that had demonstrated a commitment to the change process that had been initiated with the creation of a digital ecosystem. To build capacity, each school was matched with one central staff member and also with one teacher from another school who was already part of a learning network called *learning connections*. Learning connection teachers were taking part in a provincial learning network that supported

(Continued)

(Continued)

educators with access to applications, technology, professional learning, and collaboration opportunities. In this way we were able to gain synergies by connecting multiple learning networks. A central staff member was assigned to lead this new NPDL learning network, and she became the board champion to support and promote NPDL.

In 2015, the second year, the board built on the early successes of the NPDL learning network by expanding to 15 schools and by creating a virtual connection of five intermediate schools, for a total of 20 participating schools. Leadership from the middle became important as the work of staff involved in Year One schools was leveraged to spread the work in new schools. The model of connecting schools with one central staff member and with one teacher from another school was continued. The inquiry cycle model was used and culminated in a successful learning fair where staff celebrated and shared their successes using the NPDL framework.

An important system structure was created in that year: the central coherence committee. Senior leaders had previously encouraged interdepartmental work to try to align initiatives including the NPDL learning network. The view that function trumps structure was evident in the creation of the central coherence committee because a more nimble and strategic committee focused on coherence rather than alignment.

Capacity Building as a Priority

The capacity building that had taken place in Years One and Two was important to be able to move to the engagement of all 83 schools in Year Three. No longer would NPDL be viewed as a separate learning network, but rather it would be viewed as the board's learning and teaching framework for all learning networks. All central staff built their capacity in using the deep learning framework with a specific focus on the terminology of the four learning design elements and the six global competencies of deep learning. Learning networks such as numeracy, literacy, and kindergarten would continue, but each would use a framework of deep learning in their practice. As a Catholic school system, it was important for us to bring our religion into the definitions and approaches to teaching global competencies. Given the focus on real-life problem solving and social action, the link to Catholic graduate expectations was a seamless process.

Cultivate Action Based on Collaborative Inquiry

Each superintendent would use the school conditions rubric as a discussion point for reflecting on school innovation when they met with the school principals they supported. The existing NPDL champion would remain involved and would use her expertise to bring the deep learning process to all new teachers and to the various coaching and professional learning groups throughout the board. All staff would receive a deep learning reference guide so that they would see the language of deep learning and the coherent approach to our focus on literacy and numeracy achievement. The director of education would include deep learning as a focus in all systemwide addresses and in the monthly meeting with school principals and system leaders. Each learning network would use a rubric based on deep learning as a method for monitoring and reflecting on the system impact of their work.

Educators who were involved in Year One or Year Two of NPDL now have an opportunity to participate in a deep learning certificate program where they mentor educators from another school through an inquiry cycle, taking advantage of the toolkit of rubrics for teaching and measuring global competencies. These early adopters will be rewarded with digital badges in recognition of their work. A separate introduction to a deep learning course has been created for staff who want to accelerate their implementation of deep learning in their classrooms.

Go outside to get better inside. At the central level, we are achieving coherence because we now have departments working together and implementing their collective work using the same teaching and learning network. School staff has the same lexicon that enables them

(Continued)

(Continued)

to work collaboratively and connect learning networks. Leadership is coming from all areas of the organization, and school visits and learning walks are focusing on the four elements and six global competencies.

Ottawa Catholic has not only changed within but also offered leadership to global partners by hosting visits to their classrooms and sharing a range of resources they have created. In their own words, "Students and staff are energized with the board focus on Deep Learning. We are successfully 'using the group to move the group'" (comments by Tom D'Damico, Associate Director of OCSB, referenced in Fullan, Quinn, & McEachen, 2018, pp. 132–134).

We described at some length the OCSB district to show that large districts with good ideas and a sense of partnership can develop widespread capacity and commitment to system change at both the school and district levels. You can see from the vignette that it took a combination of district leadership and school development with close rapport between the district leadership and the school leadership, with little imposition. Deep learning is now strongly embedded in the culture of the district. It is a "system change" of some depth. It is interesting to note that a new government was elected in Ontario in June 2018, which led to budget cutbacks and little support for innovation. The new regime has had little effect on OCSB's commitment, even though it has adversely affected the budget. Strength in the middle has its own security, although our book seeks the nirvana of continuous connected autonomy within and across the three levels to form overall system change.

> By working within itself, the middle has accrued strength independent of the top.

We draw two conclusions. The first is that only a minority of districts have become successful even under supportive policy conditions (we would estimate that this represents about 25% of districts at best in North America). The future and systemwide change will require mobilizing all three levels in concert. The second conclusion and good news is that when you are successful in building ownership across a district and embedding in the culture, it may have sticking power and to a degree be resistant to harm from a more negative policy environment. Its independence strengthens precisely because it was created, understood, and embraced by the local and middle (the district in total). By working within itself, the middle has accrued strength independent of the top.

GUIDELINES FOR THE MIDDLE

At this stage we are talking about the middle as its semiautonomous self. We have not yet assembled the full picture (Chapter 5). The middle, as we have seen, has quite a set of tasks. They have to become interactive learners within their ranks—across the middle so to speak. They need to develop two-way linkages with schools below them. And they have to figure out how to contend with the agendas of those above them. We have identified seven strategies or elements within this panoply of challenges (see Figure 4.2). These components of course are similar and compatible

Figure 4.2 Successful Districts or Regions . . .

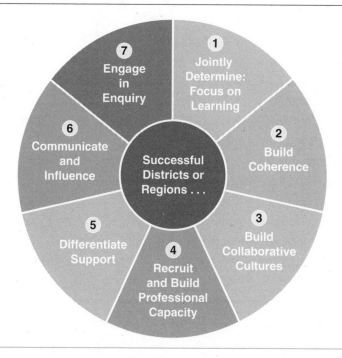

with the nine characteristics of the positive outlier districts from the LPI research. We offer them here as additional ideas to reinforce the concept of strength in the middle and to capture more of the process of development.

We should also say that the various references to districts and regions must be considered according to one's country context. In North America there are school districts, but also in many cases, regional service agencies, counties, and the like; in other countries, particularly in Europe, there are municipalities; in some, like Australia, the regions are an arm of the state government; in still others, like the Netherlands and New Zealand, there are local school councils, and recently, in the case of New Zealand, networks of schools. We think our guidelines are applicable in a variety of contexts, but, as they say in Latin, *mutatis mutandis* (make the necessary adjustments to fit the situation).

District offices become successful through a number of key roles:

1. Successful Districts Jointly Determine and Maintain Focus on Rich and Successful Learning

Successful districts keep the main thing as the main thing: Improving student learning through creating a thinking and learning system as the "North Star" (or "Southern Cross") which students use to navigate and upon which they base every decision and take every action. A neglected component of district work has been what we call "core governance" (Campbell & Fullan, 2019). Governance is a process where the direction of the organization is set, the structure is established, and accountability about fiscal and programmatic matters is assured (p. 15). Effective governance depends very much on the relationship between board trustees and superintendents. Surprisingly, there is almost no literature on this crucial relationship. Hence, our book identified five major themes of good governance: a commitment to good governance (how the organization is run); a shared moral imperative; effective trustee-superintendent relationships; school boards as coherence-makers who govern with unity of purpose; and leadership from the middle in relation to overall system change (Campbell & Fullan, 2019, p. 17). Not surprisingly (but not well known), the various successful districts we have identified all have strong superintendent-trustee relationships and corresponding good governance.

Effective districts do all of this in transparent ways so that schools can take note and follow/lead in the same direction. They constantly observe the improvement work that schools are doing, identifying and engaging those schools in sharing their "promising practices" with other schools in the district, and providing the opportunities for this sharing to take place.

A word here about "promising practices"—these are not necessarily best practices, but they may be. A promising practice is instead the next good step in learning the way forward together as a school team, a district team or a departmental team, or a vertically integrated team.

For the middle to become stronger we also need districts to learn from each other ideally involving the center as a partner as we show in Vignette 4.2.

VIGNETTE 4.2
Ontario: Learn From Peers for Your Own Good

In Ontario, when we were a few years into our successful improvements in results, we realized our system was too "top down." Some districts understood instructional leadership; others struggled. Those who struggled wanted the Ministry Student Achievement Division to tell them what to do, or wanted to avoid improvement work entirely, believing that "this too might pass" or that their district had a set of demographic challenges that meant they could not be successful. We needed district leaders to step up to the challenge and partner better with the ministry and with each other, and we needed them to focus on leadership of learning and not just good operational practices. We began a series of regional meetings of improvement teams from each district three times per year. We asked districts to include in their improvement teams for their region their director of education (superintendent in other jurisdictions), senior staff responsible for staff development, a few influential principals, and at least two teachers. We wanted to have the discussion and work center on teaching and learning and needed teachers' voices to lead the way. These meetings focused on sharing the work, successes, and challenges

(Continued)

(Continued)

among districts. When asked to present to their colleagues their "best practices" in change leadership, many districts declined, explaining they had not yet been successful enough to have a "best practice." When we asked them to tell their colleagues about their "promising practices," ideas that appeared to be moving schools forward, they all had much more to share. This also promoted the meetings as a space in which discussions of tentative ideas or even failures could be acknowledged as we were all learning together.

As districts worked within their systems to build capacity they had more to share at regional meetings. The regional meetings became more productive in the give-and-take of peers on what was being learned. In fairly short order, most districts (of the total of 72) became stronger and more effective. There were still a few weak ones—a topic we take up in Chapter 5—but overall the system got better because the middle got stronger.

Effective districts recognize that leader and staff engagement is crucial. They acknowledge and support government goals that are good for students and their learning, and they work with schools to assist them in setting school goals for change that build the school context and student needs into their local goals and targets. As the relationships develop, they also challenge all schools to set robust goals for extending student learning and engagement (goals that pursue strong foundational skill development in literacy and numeracy *and* engage students in deep learning). When they meet with school principals and school leadership teams, discussions focus on student learning, and group decisions are explained with student learning and the specific goals for students in mind. They consciously model the behaviors and priorities they advocate.

District and regional offices usually have a line or supervision responsibility with respect to the schools in their jurisdiction, or at least have some operational authority in terms of state requirements. While this might be considered wistfully as an advantage by some regional offices who don't have such a reporting relationship, it can also undermine the ability of the district to successfully deliver upon instructional leadership. When parts of the system, central departments, regional offices or districts, or even schools are accustomed to directing or being directed with respect to what and how to do what is expected, care must be taken to build a collaborative partnership of learning around the work to improve teaching and learning. The risk of falling into a top-down or directive pattern with respect to improved teaching and learning is great when it has been the norm for a relationship in the past, but this is the opposite of the culture change of what is needed to build broad system improvement.

Successful districts make "learning by staff and students" their highest and continuing priority. Operational requirements can often distract from instructional work, sometimes intentionally, often not. As an example, in the early reform work in school districts in Ontario, superintendents asked their district superintendents to visit their schools and increase the focus on instructional improvement. This of course added to an already full schedule and for some leaders it was challenging new work. Some principals equally unsure of their instructional leadership capacity tried to distract the supervisor's conversation into operational issues by first raising human relations issues, community challenges, or even capital deadlines and needs. Smart regional leaders recognized this for what it was and scheduled another meeting to talk about the operational items, protecting the conversation that was most directly linked to improving student learning in the school. And they also recognized that this was truly an expression of a learning need by the principal, namely, how to become a more effective instructional leader.

In addition, staff and student learning is featured in any regular meetings with principals and school leadership staff. Regular meetings that used to focus on administrative items or operational requirements have changed: Administrative items are reserved for communications by email or for a small part of the meeting if discussion is necessary. The largest part of the meeting, almost all in fact, is then protected for group learning around an instructional improvement agenda and for school leaders to share and learn together going forward.

2. Successful Districts Build Coherence

Coherence is described as the shared depth of understanding about the nature of the work. Alignment is rational; coherence is emotional, as we say.

You acquire coherence through shared experiences over time. It is fundamentally a change in culture (Fullan & Quinn, 2016). In successful reforms, district leaders act as "sensemakers" of the reform and its intentions, explaining, demonstrating, and asking schools to share how the various tools available to support change are connected to the overall agenda and can be embedded in the work of the school. They communicate up, down, and across the system regularly, both through formal and informal means, and promote the use of shared language as understanding is built. They ensure that any district or system resources and tools produced to support improvements to teaching and learning is consistent with the district approach and expectations placed on schools. In fact, they work to ensure that all district communications, decisions, and requirements support the critical improvement work that is taking place; and they align the district operational work to support the instructional priorities. They engage with the schools in their area and learn deeply about the schools' work, challenges, and culture. They connect schools that share common challenges with schools in the area who are more successfully working their way through the learning required to move the classroom changes along. They can make connections between central department staff and schools so that learning can be more directly connected to policy and program development at the department level. In doing these things, they are unifying the system, bringing schools to work more closely together around a shared agenda while benefiting from the supports provided by the Department of Education centrally and from the district.

Successful districts also engage laterally with other districts and regions, learning with and from each other, developing solutions to challenges. They also understand their responsibility to influence the Ministry of Education, especially those areas responsible for instructional leadership. They raise issues and challenges and recommend solutions, exploring ways to better meet the needs of schools, staff, and leaders as they move forward.

3. Successful Districts Build Purposeful Collaboration and Cultures

As researchers studied schools where improvements in student learning were taking place, it became clear even in the nineties that schools making progress had a different culture. As superintendents shared how to assess schools, one of the pieces of advice that was frequently given was that you could tell a lot about the quality of the school and learning by assessing the quality and character of the adult relationships in the building. When staff in a school knew each other, enjoyed interacting, and shared problems and solutions, students did better and demonstrated more positive attitudes toward school. While this is now seen as too superficial on its own, we know that schools that are demonstrating progress in improving student outcomes (both learning and well-being) are places in which people interact differently. Strong professional relationships and collaborative work focused on evidence-informed pedagogical decisions are the foundations of staff learning and an important part of the process through which student learning develops and is monitored, tested, and refined. The right kind of focused and open collaboration increases staff learning and provides a sense of urgency and mutual accountability for teachers to make changes in their teaching practice, monitor impact on students, and share progress and challenges. We see this clearly in the positive outlier schools and districts.

Education for decades has been based upon the privatization of teaching and claims of professional autonomy. At the heart of the cultural change that is needed to move a system forward to actually achieve improved results is the move to purposeful collaboration. Few principals today would have been part of a teaching staff in a school or system that modeled this for their leadership development. It should not be surprising that many school leaders now understand the importance of collaborative professionalism in their schools but have difficulty initiating and nurturing it.

> At the heart of the cultural change that is needed to move a system forward to actually achieve improved results is the move to purposeful collaboration.

Districts or regional offices can help make this culture shift the norm in their jurisdictions. This is not something that can be simply "mandated"; rather it is the result of district or regional staff and schools making "learning together" a visible, regular, and transparent part of how they function. While past practice may have involved most interaction between the district and a school being one on one, the attitude of "learning forward together" underpins effective district relationships in this new reality. Plans for work together with the schools in the district are developed not only keeping in mind the task to be completed but also remembering that deep staff engagement is just as important as a goal.

For example, every jurisdiction with improvement goals in mind has in place a requirement for schools to complete an annual improvement plan. And many jurisdictions require that these plans be submitted to the district or regional office or shared with the superintendent or senior staff person responsible for the school. The plans get written and filed, and the system moves on. If this "compliance mentality" is all that happens, it is at best a lost opportunity and at worst a distraction from the real change needed in the classroom. Districts need to have in place processes and relationships that allow them to be "open to learning" about the degree to which schools are successfully using the tools for planning and improving that they have available. They should be exploring with their principals and leadership teams the degree to which they are drowning in data versus analyzing and interpreting it to enable precise planning for improvement. They should be analyzing together the degree to which a school's staff is engaged in the improvement work, helping school leaders become more adept in becoming the lead learner in the school. And capacity in key areas needs to be revisited regularly as leadership teams in schools change.

Successful districts model purposeful collaboration and cultures in their own development as well. As they work with other districts and learn together, they involve school leaders in the cross-district learning and they share the learning with school leadership teams. As they work with groups of principals, they involve additional members of the school leadership teams and work to share the learning broadly in the system. They engage schools in sharing how they take advantage of the resources, including time for teachers to meet and how within the school they generate additional time for teachers to plan lessons together. They actively work to foster learning interdependency within the system in every direction and to create the conditions required for deep collaboration to take root. This is precisely what the "positive outlier" districts do, as we saw earlier in this chapter.

The end result of this deep collaborative work is that the schools that are engaged learn and improve more quickly, showing tangible and measurable improvement in student learning. And at the same time, the schools that are not engaging deeply become increasingly uncomfortable with the sense that everyone else is moving forward and they are not— fertile ground for new invitations to join in and take advantage of the growing wisdom of the group.

4. Successful Districts Recruit and Build Professional Capacity

Strong districts understand that improved learning for students is the result of improved teaching and leading by staff. Districts can access all of the resources and tools that may be available, from government or from other districts or other schools, to be used to assist schools in improving. They are more directly connected to any government or departmental entity than are the schools, so they build processes to inform and assist schools in using these resources and others to accomplish the goals for improvement that have been set.

A large part of this focus (more for Chapter 5 than here) is the development and status of the teaching profession. As the LPI study found, successful systems "develop a stable supply of well-prepared, instructionally engaged teachers and leaders" (Burns et al., 2019, p. 8). Effective districts, because they deliberately seek such teachers, and because they become known as great places to work, attract and then cultivate a strong teaching force. Of course, the system goal is to make this the norm across all schools and districts.

A district can develop the required expertise in goal setting, high impact teaching strategies, data analysis, job-embedded staff development, collaborative inquiry cycles, monitoring of impact, and leadership development. They are not likely to have in-house all of the expertise they need, however, so it is also critical that they be able to identify and access external sources of such expertise, either from a source external to the system or from within their own family of schools.

It is in this area that districts can best integrate their change leadership roles. Strong districts can bring together improvement leadership teams (principals, teachers, and in-school leaders) from all of their schools (or subsets of their schools if the district is particularly large) on a regular basis to learn together how to more effectively improve teaching and learning. These sessions should include planning time for in-school teams to move their work forward, as well as opportunities to learn new skills in change leadership from outside experts, district personnel, and other school teams as they share their learning and challenges. If structured well, these sessions can also provide schools with time and questions from a knowledgeable other acting as a critical friend to their planning: this individual could be the district liaison to their school, a different district staffer with appropriate expertise, or also a capable person from another school.

When we work with districts, a question that often arises is a concern that schools are in competition with each other for enrollment and so would not be able to develop the trusting relationship required to work together in these ways. We believe in and have seen develop in a number of jurisdictions what we call collaborative competition—a phenomenon that Hargreaves, Boyle, and Harris (2014) found in their research on high-performing organizations in sports, business, and education. Schools should compete to get better than they were and better than each other in the area that matters most to students, maximizing their learning. And most educators understand that we all have a responsibility to build success not just for the students in our own classrooms, schools, and systems, but also for those in jurisdictions around them. We should compete, but doing it by accelerating and deepening learning for our students, not by leaving other students at a disadvantage that could be overcome if we partnered better across our jurisdictions. We have found that most schools and district love to compete and learn from others who are "on the move" if the competition is centered upon improving learning with all students.

Building capacity across a system is an iterative and interactive activity. It requires constant multilevel communication. And it requires constant assessment of what staff needs to learn next or better in order to move forward with deeper student learning. Never assume that the early steps in the change process—for example, the ability to analyze, interpret, and build plans responsive to data—are in place; constantly reexamine and analyze impact on student and staff learning to find the challenges and barriers to progress. District personnel who are the liaisons to specific schools will need to meet often enough with principals of individual schools and with some of the broader school leadership team that a comfortable dialogue can take place in which the group assesses, with evidence to support, their needs for additional learning. Part of the culture that should be developed is to build into the conversations at every level a "high tolerance for the truth" as a bridge to effective improvement. In this way districts and regions learn from each other for the common good as seen in Vignette 4.3.

VIGNETTE 4.3
Regions Learn

For the past few years, I have acted as a "critical friend" to the Victoria Department of Education and Training as it moved forward with its plans for "The Education State." With each visit to Victoria, I spend time with the regional directors [there are four] and often with their staff. While I need these visits to inform my understanding of the current state of the reforms, so they are asked to include departmental program teams, school visits, some team visits and meetings, the more detailed agenda for my time is set by the regional directors. It is interesting to note that as the work together has progressed and trust has been built in our relationships, the regional directors are increasingly raising the challenges they are experiencing. We discuss the challenge, which I call the "problem of practice about particular issues," brainstorm some possible solutions, and often will co-lead a meeting of school principals, network chairs, or school-based teams in which we work together to develop potential solutions. The long-term learning from these situations comes when the regional team involved debriefs after the sessions, highlighting together what worked, what didn't work, what needs to be refined, and identifies next steps. We work actively to not only develop alternative paths to overcome the challenges but also to model the collaboration and invitations to deep thinking about change leadership that is required at all levels to build capacity (Mary Jean Gallagher, 2019).

We learned in Chapter 2 that our system model included the phrase "lateralize everywhere." What this means is that peers are the best source of learning, yet the further you go up in the system the

What this means is that peers are the best source of learning, yet the further you go up in the system the more likely you end up living in silos.

more likely you end up living in silos. What is happening in Victoria (and in Vignette 4.1 with respect to Ottawa, Ontario) is that the middle is increasingly interacting across units and regions building collaborative cultures of learning. Schools need collaborative cultures, but so do districts and regions (see Chapter 5 where we discuss the relationship between the top and the middle).

As the improvement process moves forward and more schools become master learners in creating positive impact (excellence, equity, and deeper learning) in their classrooms, districts should be looking for opportunities to increasingly engage school leaders and teachers in leadership of the continuous improvement processes across the district.

5. Successful Districts Differentiate Support and Relationships With Their Schools in Response to the School's Improvement Journey

As schools engage at different points and timing and with different levels of success with the continuous improvement processes in the region, districts will be required to increasingly differentiate their relationships and supports to schools. This requires that districts know with considerable precision where each school is and how capable they are of leading their continuous improvement cycle. And it requires to the greatest degree possible a trusting relationship between district and school personnel.

Districts should cultivate the ability to measure and respond to impact: in student learning, in staff learning, in leadership learning, and in system learning. The temptation here is to design complex and overlapping accountability systems and this would be a mistake. Layers of complex research and assessment are not what is needed here. Some of this analysis will be the result of monitoring the data the school and system use to measure impact and a lot of it will be the result of personal observations and interactions by district personnel who work most closely with the school.

In Ontario as we continued to work with school districts and school personnel throughout the reforms, government representatives and

Ministry of Education staff would repeatedly ask us how we knew districts and schools were engaged deeply and with enough precision in the reforms. We would answer that we could look at the end of the year at the improvements in measurable results that the province followed to assess impact in the goal areas, and that we could ask the districts and the schools to share with us the data and observations they had collected throughout the year to assess progress. But the earliest reliable indicators we had of where a school was and whether it would be likely to make measurable progress were the ways in which staff spoke about their learning. First of all, we would hear a difference in how teachers spoke of students who were not making progress as expected. In the old paradigm they would describe all the reasons external to the school for a student's lack of adequate progress: poverty, lack of regular attendance, new immigrant and English language learning challenges, and lack of parental engagement and support. As staff learned together how to focus on changes in the things they could control in the school to engage these students differently, we could hear their learning in their conversations: These students were struggling; a teacher would share all of the things they were working on to meet the students' learning needs; they would talk about the team and what they thought might work and why; and they would share deep excitement about the improvements they had achieved. In some cases they would state that the student had not yet improved because they, as teachers, had not yet found the way to reach them. The shift from helplessness in the face of external challenges to a growth mindset and their professional sense of efficacy would come through. We see the same shift in mindset in schools and districts with whom we work in California and in Australia. Our conclusion is that deep sustainable change across a school system happens when staff at all levels experience leading learning together. When they know they can be far more powerful in engaging students in deep and successful learning than they have been in the past, staff hold each other accountable at all levels to keep making it happen.

> Our conclusion is that deep sustainable change across a school system happens when staff at all levels experience leading learning together.

Within most districts over time a number of schools will be demonstrating solid year-over-year improvement and can articulate how they are approaching their learning and their students' deeper success—they walk the talk and talk the walk. These schools are good candidates to be paired with schools who could benefit from their example, mentoring and co-learning. District personnel visits to these schools can be less regular, still ensuring that successes are recognized and celebrated and that the school's identification of their learning needs is being attended to. With these schools, district personnel can periodically interact to ensure that schools are still actively working to develop the next level of improvement goals and plans, providing students with more deep learning opportunities and supporting an increasing spiral of staff learning together, but they will not require as much effort and time as others in the district.

Other schools in the same district will be struggling but are eager to learn and willing to work with other schools and with the district to move forward. They are curious about developing successful improvements, although they may not yet know how to lead forward and learn together with enough precision to make the difference in learning for their students. These schools will need some additional personal support and connectivity to their district but are good choices to be matched with schools with similar demographics in order to have leadership teams from both schools learn from and with each other. Victoria has created different models of pairing school and instructional supports, monitoring the impact and learning that models support in various school circumstances. We believe this approach has considerable promise as the whole system can share in this learning.

Some other schools in the district may be less engaged. They may be coasting because of complacency, believing their students are "doing fine" because the school's data compares well with other schools or with the district norms, or perhaps because they have a long-standing reputation as a "good" school. Districts need to break through this complacency in their work with these schools. Results are about improvement in student learning, and any school can and should learn to stretch and deepen their students' learning. Discussions with these schools might include comparisons to schools with similar demographics or a discussion about what value for students is added by the school's efforts. Remember, getting good grades and being good at life are not the same thing.

Finally, some schools in the district may not yet be engaged in pursuing continuous improvement. This may be a leadership problem: It is likely that they do not believe they can make progress or do not know how to begin, and they may instead be hoping that this "district or departmental fad" will pass them by. This is an opportunity for the district to move closer and intervene more regularly to assist them in moving forward. Every school does not need to be excellent (but should be striving to be), but every school should be working and over a few years making progress. The intervention should not be punitive, but it should be more consistent and persistent. In any school, effective leadership of improved teaching and learning is not an optional activity to be pursued when someone has time for it—it is the core work of the school. We describe this by saying that participating in improvement learning is invitational but inevitable, or if you prefer "voluntary but inevitable." As hesitant schools see that the work is resulting in better outcomes for students like theirs, they will become more open to partnership and resources to help them. They may in fact for the first time begin to believe it is possible for them to improve as well. It is particularly important that the district not take over ownership of the change process in the school; rather, the approach should be one of walking the journey with the school or perhaps providing a skilled leadership coach to engage with and support the principal in leading the planning and the changes. Certainly, it is appropriate for the district coach to be more specific in inquiries and discussion about what is happening, persistently expecting action to be taken at and between meetings.

In Ontario, using this approach over time we successfully reduced the number of schools identified as "low achieving" from over 750 of 4,000 elementary schools in 2005 to 63 by 2015 while at the same time expanding the definition of low achieving to intentionally include more schools in the program. It should be said here that we did not publicly identify these schools as low achieving—that kind of statement does not inspire staff to work individually and collectively to improve. Once on the move, all these schools were proud to talk about and share their new accomplishments.

While this was an initiative from the top, and thus technically should be part of Chapter 5, the goal was to strengthen districts as well as schools. All of these schools were given additional annual funding to provide resources as they worked to improve (and the only rule was that they could not spend this on additional staff). All of them already had staff who cared about their students and their learning. Almost all were schools "in challenging circumstances": Some had higher proportions of students living in poverty, while others had higher numbers of recent immigrants, or higher numbers of students living in family circumstances of strife and/or dysfunctionality. Or in some cases, some were attending schools in remote and isolated communities, where a long-term tradition of education was not established. In each case, district and regional staff worked with the schools to help them become much more precise and evidence informed about their improvement planning and actions. Each year we would bring improvement teams from these schools together to share and plan their way forward, at first regional, then at a provincial level as the numbers of schools involved became smaller. These were invariably inspiring meetings—school teams came away with renewed enthusiasm and greater clarity around what they would do to lift their own students higher.

6. Successful Districts Communicate Often (Formally and Informally) and in All Directions, Influencing Upwards and Laterally While Liberating Downwards in the System

In our model you can see that the district really is the middle communicating and working laterally within the district and with other districts, vertically with schools and enabling schools to learn from each other, and upward with state departments. Districts and regional offices become one of the main sources of information for the department or ministry with respect to the progress of the reforms in the schools. The department and the regional offices are partners in gathering evidence of impact, analyzing, and assessing how the implementation of the reforms is progressing—sharing what is working, what challenges exist, and what is needed to address these challenges. This detailed and more precise understanding of the implementation process is important input to the policy, program, and funding decisions to be made at the highest level of the system. In an implementation stage in which government must be nimble and responsive, accurate information from the front lines of the system is critical to success.

Districts also should be meeting together in their own cycles of collaborative inquiry, learning together and sharing challenges, solutions, and approaches to finding solutions. They need to work with each other and with the relevant state agencies or departments of education. System improvement requires every school and every district to be learning to improve student learning. While there is room for autonomy on the part of schools and districts, this autonomy is not isolation. They should be able to challenge each other to develop greater precision in their approaches, identifying what is working in each area and why, as well as what is not working and what can be done about it. Coherence across the system matters: in systems where significant improvements are taking place, coherence is highly visible, and staff at all levels can articulate common high-level goals and how their district or school's goals are connected to the systemwide work. There is a collaborative energy in play that can be felt—staff are able to share what they are doing to engage their students more deeply and they are pleased to do so. Where this coherence does not exist across the system, there is a greater sense of confusion: the staff wants their students to do well, but there is usually not the same level of precision in their approaches.

Consider the following scenario: Overall districts communicate throughout their own district to make sense of the changes. In order to reduce the sense of schools feeling overwhelmed by multiple initiatives, districts promote understanding of how the various supports are related to the overall goals. Research in managing change tells us that implementation proceeds more successfully if early wins are identified, celebrated, and communicated.

7. Successful Districts Explore and Engage in Inquiry About Their Own Practice and Its Efficacy

District and regional offices build their own and their schools' capacity by modeling the system implementation processes around their own goals and improvement work as well. In other words, they commit to and engage in continuous improvement. The processes that schools are expected to implement—the analysis, planning, and implementation cycles; the collaborative inquiries to shift culture and learning; the measurement and identification of impact, and the refinement of the work—are all processes that can apply equally to district goals. As districts work through the processes themselves and share their journey with their schools, they increase the focus and importance attached to the implementation activities within the district. They learn about the nuances, challenges, and efficacy of the work. They also model the importance of the processes in building rigor, and they model the actions that flow from the analysis and the planning. Within this context, districts can also be effective at helping struggling schools to turn around, as we see in Vignette 4.4

VIGNETTE 4.4
Turnaround Schools

When Ontario began its improvement journey I was the director [superintendent] of Ontario's southernmost school district. One of my schools was identified by the ministry as a "low achieving school," eligible for its first version of its program of assistance "Turnaround Schools." The ministry sent an external diagnostician to the school every six to eight weeks to help the staff identify what needed to change, and it provided funds for substitute teachers to allow teachers in each division of the school to meet with the diagnostician for half a day of planning. As director of the system, I knew we had already supported this school and a few others to try to turn around their results with some of our students living in the most challenged circumstances—we had provided extra staff, some of our best principals and teachers, more social work and psychological assistance, additional diversity of staff to reflect the diversity of the student population, extra staff professional learning time, lunch and breakfast programs, and extra budget to respond to other student needs—but we were not seeing the results in student testing and teacher observation of their skills in key areas. I was pleased the ministry had selected one of these schools in my system as we felt we had tried everything. The day after the ministry diagnostician visited the school and worked with the staff, as director/superintendent of the district (a large system with 75 schools), I visited the school at lunchtime. I arranged a catered lunch for the staff and sat with them. We had no specific agenda. I told them that I was very interested in learning what they were learning, so that I could help some of our other schools become more successful too. I thanked them for the effort they were making to improve their students' learning.

Each visit I asked them how they were feeling about the process, what they had been doing the previous day, and what they might be doing differently over the next two months. As time went on, the discussion became livelier and more authentic. Each month I would report on what was happening at this school to all the rest of my school principals. Staff in all of my schools came to understand my commitment to the importance of improvement and my belief that if we learned together, we could do it successfully. Provincewide almost all of the schools in this program improved, but as soon as the diagnostician stopped coming to help, most of them sank back down over the next few years. By this time, I was leading the Student Achievement Division for the ministry and carried responsibility for this program. Combining my "on the ground" learning with the strong research and policy development skills of ministry staff allowed us to redesign the program for greater success in subsequent years. We removed the external diagnosticians and provided a "coach or critical friend" to help the school staff learn to identify their own challenges of practice and responses through the use of a robust and action-oriented school improvement planning process. We worked with schools as they focused on a combination of initial improvement, links to the district's role in supporting continuous improvement, and schools learning from each other (Mary Jean Gallagher, 2019).

If schools in their district share a common challenge to which the solution is not known or easily adapted, these districts take advantage of the opportunity to bring schools together to think, learn, generate hypotheses, and develop plans to test potential solutions. They learn with their schools in these meetings, demonstrating the efficacy of focused thinking and precision in implementation of alternative solutions. These sessions can become opportunities to engage school staff in the work more effectively. Most importantly, in these sessions districts will improve in their ability to lead the changes throughout their district and strengthen the culture of professional curiosity and precision in classroom implementation. In sum, when we consider the middle, change in the culture of the district and its schools is the unit of change.

CONCLUSION

It is the work of the districts and regional offices that holds the key to making educational improvement a systemwide phenomenon. As we discuss in Chapter 5, governments understand and work with five levers for change: legislation, regulation, policy, program, and funding. Such a culture drives their perspective of the education system and their view of the nature of the work required to build systemic change. These things are needed in the right combination around the right drivers to build conditions favorable to continuous improvement in our school system. But policies from the top will not by themselves be able to create a culture of thoughtful, evidence-informed continuous improvement in learning across thousands of classrooms. To a certain extent, entities in the middle (districts and regions) need to develop their own capacity to lead improvement. They need to learn this by getting to understand local cultures (Chapter 3) and government cultures (Chapter 5) as part and parcel of figuring out their own roles.

In this chapter we are addressing the middle as a semiautonomous layer of the system. Since we are stressing that each layer should work to enlarge its own sense of autonomous action, we recommend that the middle learn from itself. The middle could begin by asking the following questions: What do other units in the middle do? How can we learn from each other? How do we contend with the vagaries of policy? How can we foster a culture of accountability below us? Welcome to life in the middle!

The changes needed in schools today are huge and intimidating—requiring wholesale and deep change in content and culture in school systems, focused on excellence, equity, and well-being in both foundational skills and deep learning. Any actual improvements are achieved at the school and community levels. External motivation cannot and does not work. New research in motivation and learning confirms that purpose, mastery, autonomy, and connectedness drive intrinsic motivation (this is true by the way for staff and students, offering us a way forward in reversing our students' disengagement with education). These same factors define professionalism in many fields. This means that the successful path forward rests with educators focused on their deep moral purpose of lifting all students to their personal and most richly imagined futures, preparing our students to successfully change their world. It asks that teachers thoughtfully decide upon the pedagogy to be used in their classrooms in response to the learning goals of the day. It requires that teachers become master educators who constantly inquire about better ways to teach, and for their students to learn approaches that are based upon excellent research being put into practice so the impact can be identified and further refinements made. No one can do this in isolation, but it can be done. Schools and their culture can make the difference by building with staff a powerful sense of efficacy in their professional practice.

Schools cannot do this alone, but groupings of schools can. Districts or other regional clusters can support, encourage, and embed their schools within a culture of deep purpose, where ideas and challenges are shared, resulting in greater impact on learning for staff and students. Once such a culture is created and continues to be nurtured, mastery for students and staff becomes the most probable outcome.

Sounds good, doesn't it? But still, we have one more stop on our journey—to get to the top itself.

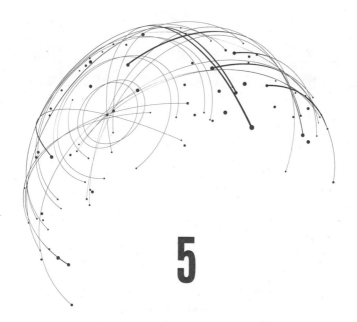

5

The Macro
Direction and Liberation

· ·

Our goal in this chapter is not to provide a full model of system reform. Rather it is to make three critical points about the policies, strategies, and mindset needed for successful systemwide reform. First, the challenge of system change and education's role therein has become qualitatively different in recent times. We need a new mindset to accomplish new system change. Second, the models we have worked with in Ontario, California, and Victoria furnish good examples of works in progress but

> If details are increasingly mounting and characterized by nonlinearity, how do you contend with them? Our argument in this book is that you need layered, connected autonomy.

do not yet take us fully to the new destination. Third, we return to our conception of a trilevel system that addresses the devil in the details in the service of transforming the system for the better.

New System Challenges; New Mindsets

1. In the early 2000s we made some progress in designing policies and strategies that supported stronger implementation and obtained better results (in Ontario, for example). We got better and better at capacity building.

2. As in other fields of system change, we began to reach the limits of complexity control. The world was becoming more complex, the dynamics of change embodied more variables, feedback systems ramified, and surprising developments occurred, all of which resembled complex adaptive systems whose actions could not be predicted in advance. Think of climate change, technology, and jobs and recall Morieux and Tollman's study (2014) from Chapter 2 that found "business complexity" (structures, rules, and roles) had increased sixfold since 1955.

3. As the environment became more challenging, the goals for change in education became more complex, going beyond literacy to dealing with living in uncertain and dangerous times. The fundamental goals of equity, excellence, and well-being became increasingly urgent aspirations. Best systems aspire to all three as a synergistic force to improve the lives of all, individually and collectively. Learning and engagement by all becomes crucial.

4. In this context, inevitably policy from the top reached its limits— complexity has yielded to complicatedness. New paradigms were required but not yet developed.

"Beyond complexity" means more and more unpredictable details. If details are increasingly mounting and characterized by nonlinearity, how do you contend with them? Our argument in this book is that you need layered, connected autonomy. Since each level in ultracomplex systems inevitably has degrees of autonomy, whether we like it or not, why not make it a virtue? Look for ways to develop capacity at each level, respect autonomy in exchange for a commitment to interact (laterally and vertically), and ensure that interaction and evidence-informed action occur around the right agenda: the moral purpose of equity, excellence, and well-being, and capacities therein, leading to becoming better at life in complex times.

We must return to the concept of "details." Details are neither intrinsically good nor bad. Presumably if they are associated with the devil, they are bad. If variegated details are inevitable (and in our beyond complexity world, they are guaranteed to multiply inexorably), how do we maximize their use? We use leadership, broadly conceived to capture this. When it comes to details, *context* is everything. In *Nuance* (2019) Fullan found that successful leaders were indeed experts in context. They spent a great deal of time "participating as learners," interacting with those at their own level and also with those at other levels. John Malloy, director of education of the Toronto District School Board (TDSB), is a case in point. With 583 schools and massive complexity and politics, John spends a great deal of time working alongside his 30 or so central leaders visiting schools and learning what is happening. In this way these central leaders get to know more, and more, and more.

> Since each level in ultracomplex systems inevitably has degrees of autonomy, whether we like it or not, why not make it a virtue?

Second, Malloy and his team give a good degree of autonomy to schools, helping them to develop capacity for implementing practices that get results. They are using our principle of "liberating" those below you, but they are liberating "groups," not individuals. They develop social and decisional capital as well as human capital (Hargreaves & Fullan, 2012). The principle is "trust and interact," interacting all the time, but intervening only when there are serious problems to be addressed. If you trust and interact, you learn what is going on—in a phrase you learn more details. But it is impossible to know and to control everything, so you have to invest in others so that they too learn in context and act successfully even when you are not on the scene—which, of course, is most of the time.

Even this explanation is incomplete, and we will in the course of this chapter use three big systems that we work with—Ontario, California, and Victoria—to learn more detail about how learning in context can be strengthened through the actions taken at the top. We consider these three jurisdictions very good systems that are heading in the right direction (with Ontario being a current, and we would predict temporary, exception due to a reversal of policy direction arising from an election in June 2018).

In the meantime, here is the firm conclusion. Good systems get at detail both *directly* (they spend time learning as much as they can about local and middle levels in action) and *indirectly* (but nonetheless explicitly)—through human, social, and decisional capital investments. Such systems foster the capacity to deal with detail at the other levels. The overall effect is that the system becomes good at knowing and dealing with detail. And once these details are organized to operate in your favor, *god* is in the details as the system operates at a high level of performance. We trust that the reader accepts that we are using devil and god metaphorically; it is humans who are changing our destiny by design or neglect.

> These days you have to treat implementation as a *learning proposition,* not as a matter of executing policy.

As part of developing the new mindset, the first order of business for policy makers (politicians and bureaucrats) is to read Chapter 3 and reflect on what life is like at the local level; same for the middle, Chapter 4. The goal is not to plan directly from that knowledge but to be sensitized to the other two worlds that you don't inhabit. Double up on this knowledge by visiting and talking to people on a continuous basis at each of the other two levels. Become greater experts at understanding contexts.

When Fullan wrote the first edition of *The Meaning of Educational Change* (1982), he had this to say:

> Government agencies have been preoccupied with program adoption. Until recently they vastly underestimated the processes of implementation. We have a classic case of two entirely different worlds—the policy maker on the one hand and the practitioner on the other hand. To the extent that each side is ignorant of the *subjective world* of the other, reform will fail, and the extent is great. (p. 74, italics in the original)

Almost four decades later we would say that policy makers do have a greater appreciation of implementation, but they do not as easily grasp the complexity argument we have offered in this book: Things are too complex to control from the top. These days you have to treat implementation as a *learning proposition*, not as a matter of executing policy. The dynamics of learning and its feedback loops and iterations govern the success at each level and their interaction.

The worlds of policy and local living are indeed two different worlds. This was starkly brought home when one of us switched from the role of district leader to government leader in the Ministry of Education in Ontario (Vignette 5.1).

VIGNETTE 5.1
Divergent Worlds

Gallagher: I had the opportunity twice in my career to move from the role of director (or superintendent of a school district) to chief executive officer in the Ministry of Education and eventually to assistant deputy minister of education in government. Both times, after about two months in my new job, I found myself in my office late at night in tears, convinced I had made the biggest mistake of my life. Too many of my new colleagues in government service didn't know how to make anything happen, they moved too slowly, they didn't understand what really mattered, and they were so risk averse, they seemed happier to have nothing happen than to take action! Both times I was at risk of joining the bandwagon that "government and its agencies are incompetent" and thinking of myself as above that level. But then I took a step back. I intentionally adopted an "open to learning" stance. I hired one of the smartest government thinkers I could find since I knew I needed to become more effective in my role, as school reform in Ontario depended on building a more productive relationship between the ministry and the field. I began to understand that both government and the school system had developed cultures and processes perfectly suited to deliver their own success and unwittingly their failures, and I developed an appreciation

(Continued)

(Continued)

for the strengths of many more of my colleagues. I also began to look for ways where each level could learn about the other's culture. We adopted a practice of "seconding" local district personnel for periods of time into our government agency, after which they would return to their districts. After a while you could always find people at the district level who had worked at the ministry, and of course district people would find people in the ministry who had worked recently in districts. And most importantly they worked successfully together. Relationships across the two levels improved immensely as a result of this practice.

Whole system change is often set as a goal at the top of the system, with the government and its agencies or ministries responsible for education within the nation or state. In one sense, government should be an extension of the desires of parents, citizens, and business to plan for a successful and healthy future for our children, our communities, and our economies. Government, supported by the Ministry or Department of Education, has the responsibility to determine the architecture of the system, and it has the authority to establish the goals of the education system (core priorities), including the broad goals for improvement. They determine the curriculum (the expectations of the system in terms of what students are expected to learn, to know, to do, and to understand) and identify the level of performance or achievement by the student that is expected. They also have responsibility for resourcing it in support of the goals they set (see Figure 5.1).

At the outset, systemwide improvement in education begins with the identification of something that needs to improve in the school system. In democracies government agenda are supposed to be a reflection of the will of the people, but there is a great deal of complexity and interpretation involved. Most governments, we think it is accurate to say, are not great at implementation, which, in a perverse way, is a good thing because they often choose the wrong pathways. The potentially good news is that the focus on systemwide change and how to achieve it has become a priority

Figure 5.1   The Top

over the past decade and a half. Thus, much of the knowledge base we draw on has been formulated since about 2000.

One of the positive results is the focus on data in most education systems. More goals can now be set based upon evidence about student learning as well as aspirations for what students need to know, understand, and be able to do in preparation for a successful future. This then can become the highest-level example of the importance of detail, as increased precision and evidence being used to move the system forward, both in establishing relevant goals and in monitoring whether a particular change or approach is effective.

Governments generally have five levers through which they can cause change: legislation, regulation, policy, program, and funding. These approaches work particularly well when a problem or challenge is a technical one, one in which the solution can reasonably be known or designed. These government levers can be very successful when it comes to defining and specifying the minimum standard of compliance in a system. They can, for example, require a minimum entry standard for aspiring teachers to enter pre-service preparation. The five levers frame and guide direction, but they can never be sufficient when it comes to quality action on the ground. Things become more complex when the solution to the challenge requires front line staff to learn the way forward, developing and refining the solution as they address the challenge. In this scenario, legislation, regulation, and policy are particularly ill-suited to effect change; at best they might establish a minimum standard in terms of processes and conditions to be used to address the issue, but this provides no guarantee of real progress. For example, in the pursuit of improved teaching and learning in schools, a government may be able to use regulation or policy to establish a requirement that schools complete an annual improvement plan. This is in fact one of the basic building blocks in support of smart system reform. But all too often the plan becomes a complex document that complies with government or departmental direction and becomes an end unto itself. Schools or districts spend precious time producing a document for the sake of compliance, and it all has little or no impact on what action the school might actually take to effect improvement or what teachers actually might do differently in a classroom with their students.

Even when intentions are good, things go awry. In California, which we consider to have a very good policy framework, there is a requirement that districts write an annual LCAP (Local Control Accountability Plan). The idea was that districts would have local freedom and more resources than ever before, and "little old" LCAP would be the accountability requirement. The trouble was that the county offices (historically a bureaucratic chain in the system) had little experience with local autonomy, and they began to require specific modifications in the plans. The result was that many districts found themselves with plans of 300 pages or more. No one wanted this as an outcome. It just crept in as a result of bureaucratic habits. The system responded to rectify the problem, but it took some four years to alleviate a situation that almost no one favored.

System improvement in the new LCAP culture cannot be achieved directly through usual levers through which government institutions work. In combination, such levers are necessary to set the stage and create conditions, which can act as a catalyst to engage school staff in deep improvement work. Governments, in order to lean in and have real improvement take place across the system, must move beyond legislation, regulation, and most policy work very early in the reform journey. They must learn to use the tools of programming and funding in new ways to stimulate action at the middle and local levels that treats implementation as a collaborative learning phenomenon. This includes creating, partnering with, and supporting the middle layers of regions and districts to lead the system through the deep details of implementation—the kind of work we saw evidenced in the "positive outlier" districts in Chapter 4.

The work and the learning at every level of the system is about creating culture change in a wide range of schools. Leading such a broad and complex change requires adaptive, interactive leadership and decision-making, open communications up, down, and all across the system, a receptivity to learning the way forward, and a disposition to collaborate. With the right mindset, through interaction with the other levels, and the tools, supports and requirements put in place, the top ends up influencing the other levels *indirectly but nonetheless explicitly* with respect to the student learning agenda. In the best cases a growing sense of partnership evolves between the center and other levels.

With this context in mind we can turn to real examples of whole system reform. We are intimately associated with three such cases in three different countries. All three jurisdictions (Ontario's current diversion notwithstanding) are on the right track and promise to go further in representing the system transformation that we are examining in this book. Figure 5.2 furnishes a profile of the three jurisdictions.

Figure 5.2   Reform Profiles

Ontario, Canada	California, United States	Victoria, Australia
System		
• 2,000,000 students • 4,900 schools • 72 districts	• 6,300,000 students • 10,700 schools • 1,009 districts • 58 counties	• 630,000 students • 1,600 schools • 4 regions
Timeline		
2003–2018	2013–present	2015–present
Goals		

• Literacy
• Numeracy
• High school graduation
• Public confidence
	• 8 state priorities:
	  o Basic services
	  o Standards
	  o Parental involvement
	  o Pupil achievement
	  o Pupil engagement
	  o School climate
	  o Course access
	  o Others
		• Excellence
		• Equity
		• Well-being
		• 10 goal areas

(Continued)

(Continued)

Ontario, Canada	California, United States	Victoria, Australia
Early Learning		
• Expanded full day kindergarten for 4- and 5-year-olds	• Expanded preschool • Enhanced 0–5 development	• Kindergarten for 3-year-olds • Differentiated school readiness funding to pursue equity
Leadership		
• Dedicated division within Ministry of Education • Additional senior staff for districts • Additional secondary school teacher to implement student success programs • Strategic engagement of all levels	• Transition of state agencies (CDE, CCEE, counties) • Local Control Funding Formula (LCFF) • Establishment of some networks for lateral learning • Initial development of statewide system of support	• Learning places: expanded role and enhanced staffing in regions • Expanded role for central department teams • Principal networks • School-based instructional leadership staff
Planning Tools		
• District effectiveness framework • School effectiveness framework • School improvement plan	• Local Control and Accountability Plan (LCAP)	• Annual Improvement Plans • School review process • Framework for Improving Student Outcomes (FISO)
Capacity Building		
• Effective pedagogy • Instructional leadership • Monographs and videos • Multiple lateral learning strategies (LSA, TLLP) • Specific content resources	• District leadership in response to teacher need • Established new agency to support implementation: California Collaborative for Education Excellence • Shifted county role from compliance to capacity building	• Expanded role for Bastow Institute for professional learning • High Impact Teaching Strategies (HITS) • Professional learning networks • Videos • Student engagement support (AMPLIFY) • Specific content resources (LIT, NUM)

Ontario, Canada	California, United States	Victoria, Australia
Data Monitored		
• Annual literacy and numeracy results in provincial testing (Grades 3, 6, 9, and 10) • Graduation rates • Credit accumulation rates	• California School Dashboard (status and improvement)	• Annual results in national test (NAPLAN years 3, 5, 7, and 9) • Attendance • Student well-being survey results • Improvement plans
Results		
• Literacy and numeracy results improved 17% • Graduation results improved 19% • Weaker results in mathematics • Increase in school and district capacity • Significant gains in public confidence	• Increased student achievement in some districts • Reduced suspension rates • Closing equity gaps in some districts; large gaps remain • Higher graduation rates and eligibility for university • Significant gain in Grade 8 reading • Rate of improvement higher than national	• Leads the country in 7 of 10 indicators • Increased proportion of primary students (years 3 and 5) in top levels in literacy and numeracy • Fewer primary students in lower levels in literacy and numeracy • Significant improvements in year 7 • Strong policies; need greater implementation

Now to the details.

....

ONTARIO, CANADA; CALIFORNIA, UNITED STATES; VICTORIA, AUSTRALIA: GOOD START-UPS AT DIFFERENT PLACES IN THE LEARNING

....

We are not suggesting that other jurisdictions are failing to make progress on system reform (see O'Day & Smith, 2019; Schliecher, 2018; and Tucker, 2019). But we don't think that these and other models in the literature adequately take into account the dynamics of trilevel reform. By contrast, Ontario, California, and Victoria are all examples of systems that have been making direct attempts at whole system transformation over the last decade (as we noted, Ontario has faltered recently, but that does not alter our argument here). The three systems represent strong models of system reform and are making good progress but have not yet achieved full success, while two of the three continue to refine and alter what they are doing. They are not necessarily exemplars, but they do represent impressive cases of the evolution of complexity and proactive system responses.

Ontario

Ontario has a population of 14.5 million with a highly diverse multicultural makeup (half the population of Toronto was born outside Canada). In 2002, the Ontario system was flatlined or stagnant in terms of literacy and high school graduation rates, and had been since 1998. A newly elected government began a reform effort in 2003 focusing on its 4,900 schools (4,000 elementary and 900 secondary schools, and two million students). A word on full disclosure: Fullan served as senior adviser to the premier, Dalton McGuinty, and Gallagher became assistant deputy minister of the Literacy and Numeracy Secretariat and Student Success during this reform period.

The reform stated three priorities: to excel in literacy, math, and high school graduation; raise the bar and lower the gap in these three areas; and increase public confidence in the public school system. From 2004 to 2017 Ontario achieved rapid and continuing success on two measures—literacy and high school graduation—and, if we could measure it, major developments in individual capacity and collective capacity for bringing about change (math is another matter, too complex to take up here). We have written elsewhere about the Ontario success story (Fullan & Rincón-Gallardo, 2016). Here we give a brief account of the main strategies that consisted of eight interrelated components. The reader will recognize that the list is similar to those factors identified in Figure 1.2. The difference is minimal and arises because the earlier version covers the period up to 2010, whereas the current list is updated to 2016.

1. A small number of ambitious goals (high standards and expectations) relentlessly pursued: literacy, numeracy, high school graduation,

reduction of learning gaps, and increased public confidence. Along the way (in 2010) Ontario also established full-day kindergarten for all four- and five-year-olds.

2. A focus on leadership and capacity building related to effective pedagogy that included developing school principals as lead learners, adding School Effectiveness and Student Success Leaders at each of the districts, and Student Success Teachers (SST) at the secondary level (one SST per district, $N = 7\,2$, and one per school, $N = 900$).

3. Establishing a new unit within the Ministry of Education to include the Literacy Numeracy Secretariat (LNS) and the Student Success branch whose staff included a number of skilled practitioners from both the school system and government who worked jointly with school districts to build their focus and capacity on the core goals.

4. Mobilizing data and intervention in a nonpunitive manner, reducing distractions, and establishing principles of trust, transparency, and urgency thereby examining progress and designing related actions at every level of the system.

5. Strategic actions taken to engage every level of the system—building coherence at classroom, school district, and provincial levels—including structures and professional resources (materials, time) to support staff analysis, planning, and action in response to each school's needs. A heavy emphasis was placed on engaging pedagogies such as collaborative inquiry and its links to student engagement and achievement.

6. Using mutually reinforcing overlapping strategies to learn from and within the system *during implementation*. These include focused provincial and regional meetings to share ideas about what works best in practice relative to each priority; funding a strategy called Leading Student Achievement (LSA), which is carried out by the three school principals' associations; and developing another initiative named Teaching Learning and Leadership Program (TLLP), funded by the government and organized by the teacher unions in which two or more teachers apply for funds to examine issues of

practice related to policy priorities and for which they report back to peer groups conducting other TLLP studies, and to the general field through conferences and professional publications (Campbell, Leiberman, & Yashkina, 2015).

7. Throughout this we see the emergence of leadership from the middle (LftM) that we discussed in Chapter 4, in which districts develop greater intradistrict capacity and interdistrict networks of learning and become better partners to schools and upwards to the province.

8. Investment of resources both in terms of the base budget and in relation to targeted funding of strategies that addressed the needs of those doing less well in the system.

These strategies were designed to build capacity. And they did get at detail. The combination of focus and related vertical and lateral capacity building therein mobilized "the details" to work in favor of system reform. All of this targeted capacity building was continually reinforced through regional and provincial sessions in which progress was examined and effective strategies and lessons for success were shared.

Another key element of the reform was to establish a student data and evidence tracking system. Any improvement plan begins with an analysis of where the system is at present and the ability to judge whether and how it is improving over time. To complete this analysis, a student data system must be established, robust enough to examine changes in student learning and achievement over time on a variety of indicators (especially those related to improvement goals). It should allow tracking of cohorts of students longitudinally over a student's education pathway, as well as permit the disaggregation of data into student groupings that would allow a department of education to identify student groups in need of specific strategies as well as the relative efficacy and impact of those strategies on learning. Over time, decisions at the government level can then increasingly be based on evidence of what works well in increasing impact on students and learning.

Improving student learning, increasing their success over time, is a complex undertaking. Any data system at the macro or state level should include a number of different indicators of student progress and it should be realized that analysis of this data produces trends and possible inter-pretations, not hard conclusions. It points the way to further analysis to inform decisions. A data system that is too narrowly focused may become a driver for an education system that is too limited, cheating students of an opportunity for a broad, comprehensive education and one that engages them in a lifetime of learning (not to mention that a narrow curriculum alienates many students). But a tracking system that does not include some common measures across the system makes learning what works across the system more difficult.

Ideally a data system should include teacher assessments of student learning (marks and observations of growth over time), student results on state or provincewide testing over time, and student program enrollment data and other student data that may be related to achieving the desired and stated outcomes. This may include attendance records, student sur-vey responses to questions about levels of interest and engagement in schooling or questions related to well-being, programs in which a stu-dent is enrolled, and any demographic or program data that may assist the system in understanding and addressing student needs. It should also support decision-making regarding areas in which programs and tools for staff development may be needed. Vignette 5.2 provides an example of evidence-based use with respect to the Ontario reform.

VIGNETTE 5.2
Learning to Use Evidence

Over time Ontario was able to track a student's pathway from his or her Early Learning program to elementary and secondary school and on to postsecondary programs. This produced rich data for schools and for the Ministry of Education to use to improve the system. For example, when a student in high school enrolled in a particular group of courses related to a potential career interest (Specialist High Skills Major [SHSM] was one such program designed to encourage

(Continued)

(Continued)

students to see the relevance of their high school program to a potential career area), the ministry or its research teams could track the proportion of students who went on to graduate from high school and enroll at a postsecondary destination related to their secondary school specialization. This allowed decisions about program enhancements and additional funding investments to be more precisely targeted, ensuring program expansions took place in areas where demand and success were greater and program refinements could be targeted where students were not as successful. This tracking information was shared widely with district staff responsible for the SHSM programs, and it set the stage for robust discussions at every level about challenges to be resolved. The result of this and other changes has been a major and steady increase in high school graduation from 68% in 2003 to the current 88% across the 900 secondary schools in the province.

The overall Ontario system change model described was effective for achieving system change that was fairly complex; but it is not sufficient for the new "beyond complexity" situation with which we opened this chapter. For one thing society changed and has become more complex and dangerous—educated citizens of the present need to become much more than literate to manage, let alone thrive.

And policy was changing (as it should). In Ontario a new premier, Kathleen Wynne, was elected (same political party) and after consultation introduced a new policy platform called Achieving Excellence (Ontario, 2014). It endorsed the existing goals of excellence in literacy and numeracy, narrowing the gaps and public confidence, but expanded one existing priority (equity) and added one big new priority (well-being).

As they say, this was a game changer. It also coincided with another development that favored a change in strategy. In the course of capacity building in the 2004–2014 phase, districts and their schools got stronger. In the early part of the reform, although it was not expressed in these words, the government developed district capacity so that it could implement the government priorities, which many educators also believed in.

But guess what? When you develop new capacity, people or groups soon start to think for themselves. Instead of implementing "your agenda" (from the top, for example), they begin to have ideas of their own. In so doing they can also become potentially better partners upward to government, and/or with their schools. Eventually, many districts saw their own greater capacity as beneficial for formulating their own priorities, albeit in the context of system policy. This brings us full circle to the premise of this book: society and education are so complex that we need degrees of autonomy at each level that serves to contribute to the overall solution.

> Society and education are so complex that we need degrees of autonomy at each level that serves to contribute to the overall solution.

As far as Ontario is concerned—and virtually everywhere else—it doesn't yet know how to effectively integrate excellence, equity, and well-being. Ontario got a good start in 2014 by building on its LftM strength and pursuing deep learning in several districts. In 2018, Ontario even got as far as proposing that the 6Cs be the basis of school report cards. Consideration was underway of creating greater opportunity within curriculum and school policy processes for more integrated studies and student-led programs. But alas, the election of a new party and populist government in 2018 halted all official action related to the existing (2018) agenda, replacing it with a platform to make massive budget cuts in education and elsewhere, and with no content vision or agenda.

In Ontario, the 2019 budget cuts have been made. These are too numerous to list and, in some cases, to capture, since the government has partially backtracked on many of them. These cuts include reducing the teaching force by 10,000 teachers through increased class size, a full semester of compulsory e-learning, less funding for autism, and reduction of funding in a whole range of supports for students, families, and support agencies. Massive protests and "work to rule" are underway from students, support staff, community groups, and teachers. In the fall of 2019, 98% of the members of the two largest teacher unions voted to give their leaders the mandate to call a strike.

Our own view, which as you can imagine is not neutral, is that the strength of the education system that developed from 2004 to 2018 makes it less likely that the system will reverse what has been gained. It is not just that the districts will resist a reversal of strategy, but also because the students and communities represent powerful change forces, which, if linked with district leadership, would be formidable. In other words, local school communities and districts can use their learnings over the past decade to the advantage of students even in challenging political times.

Time will tell—perhaps a short time since the situation is volatile. In any case, we see in Ontario great potential for moving into "deep learning" that integrates excellence, equity, and well-being (see Fullan et al., 2018, and Quinn et al., 2020, for details of "deep learning" in action in several jurisdictions including Ontario). This potential for deep learning exists because the floor of capacity building among educators in the province is quite solid, and the learning needs of young people are falling increasingly far short of what is required—and they know it!

California

California is the fifth largest economy in the world (recently passing the United Kingdom) with a population of about 40 million, some 10,700 schools in 1,009 districts and 58 counties. We have worked in California for some time, and for the last six years, funded by the Stuart Foundation, we have been supporting and studying the California reform that began in 2012. Our latest report is: *California's Golden Opportunity: Learning Is the Work* (Fullan, Rincón-Gallardo, & Gallagher, 2019).

Governor Jerry Brown was elected in 2010 and introduced a radical reform in 2013 called Local Control Funding Formula (LCFF), along with a requirement for each district to produce an annual Local Control Accountability Plan (LCAP). The plan, known as "The California Way," shifted billions of dollars to local districts serving high-needs students and empowers districts, in partnership with local communities and schools, to develop plans in relation to local priorities. These structural changes coincided with the state's implementation of the Common Core State Standards and the Smarter Balanced Assessment System. The philosophy of the reform followed the Ontario design of de-emphasizing punitive accountability and focusing on "assess, support and improve" through collaboration and capacity building (see Furger, Hernandez, & Darling-Hammond, 2019). In addition, other policies are focusing on the compensation, preparation, and support of new teachers, expansion of early childhood programs, and more.

The state also created the California School Dashboard. The dashboard is an online tool showing the status and progress of schools and districts with respect to state priorities. It is designed as an open-ended tool expected to be continuously improved and refined over time. Staff in California's districts appreciate the fact that the second iteration of the tool is improved, saying it is much easier to understand and the data is available in a more timely fashion. It includes multiple measures of status and progress on the eight state priorities for all students and for a number of student subgroups. This increases its potential for differentiated use but makes it a more complicated document to use. Like most data, what determines success is not so much the data itself but rather the importance of learning to interpret and use the information wisely, along with the associated capacities that we are discussing in Chapters 3 through 5.

The eight state priorities are portrayed in Figure 5.3, California's State Priorities.

From a strategy perspective, progress depends on a complex array of actors, including the State Board, the California Department of Education (CDE), the 58 county offices, the recently established (2013) support agency, the California Collaborative for Education Excellence (CCEE), and the 1,009 independent districts and 10,700 schools. *Talk about details!* We pointed out in one of our earlier California reports that the reform assumed that providing districts and schools with more authority and resources would be the key to success, but the reformers failed to realize that many districts did not have the capacity to take advantage of the opportunity. Thus, the scramble over the past eight years has been to help build local capacity—a mammoth undertaking given the wide range of districts in terms of numbers and conditions, along with the layers of agencies in the state.

The evolving system of support, nonpunitive basis notwithstanding, is a labyrinth of complicatedness (see Figure 5.4).

Despite the sheer number of moving pieces, there is a good deal of capacity building expertise in the system, which we can call "leadership from the middle," that is being mobilized for district and school capacity building. We reported in Chapter 4 on the assessment of "positive outliers" carried out by the Learning Policy Institute (LPI). One report consisted of a quantitative analysis of how districts of poverty were performing (using

Figure 5.3 California's State Priorities

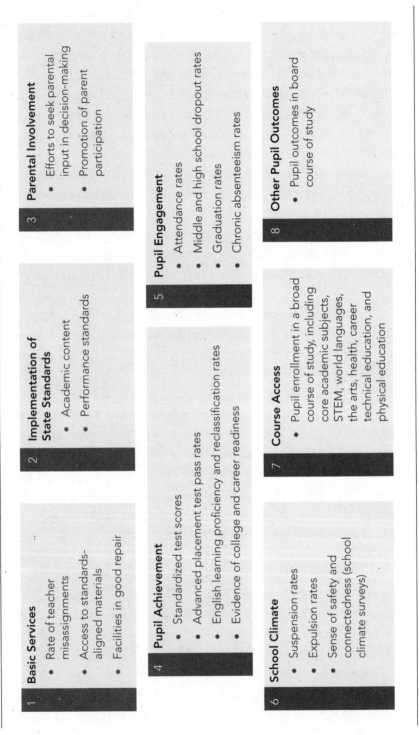

1 Basic Services
- Rate of teacher misassignments
- Access to standards-aligned materials
- Facilities in good repair

2 Implementation of State Standards
- Academic content
- Performance standards

3 Parental Involvement
- Efforts to seek parental input in decision-making
- Promotion of parent participation

4 Pupil Achievement
- Standardized test scores
- Advanced placement test pass rates
- English learning proficiency and reclassification rates
- Evidence of college and career readiness

5 Pupil Engagement
- Attendance rates
- Middle and high school dropout rates
- Graduation rates
- Chronic absenteeism rates

6 School Climate
- Suspension rates
- Expulsion rates
- Sense of safety and connectedness (school climate surveys)

7 Course Access
- Pupil enrollment in a broad course of study, including core academic subjects, STEM, world languages, the arts, health, career technical education, and physical education

8 Other Pupil Outcomes
- Pupil outcomes in board course of study

Source: California Department of Education. Furger, Hernández, & Darling-Hammond, 2019 (CC BY-NC 4.0)

Figure 5.4   California Statewide System of Support

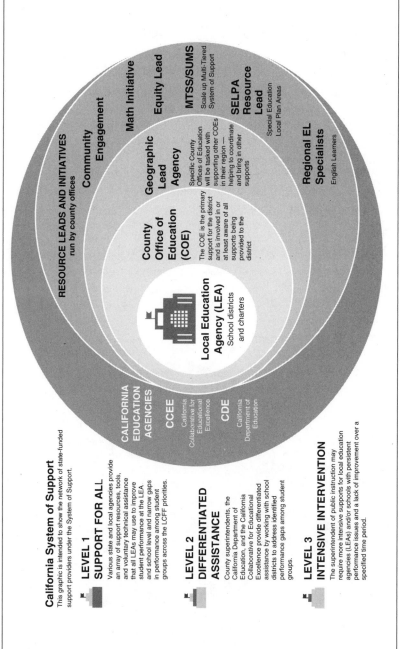

California System of Support
This graphic is intended to show the network of state-funded support providers under the System of Support.

LEVEL 1
SUPPORT FOR ALL
Various state and local agencies provide an array of support resources, tools, and voluntary technical assistance that all LEAs may use to improve student performance at the LEA and school level and narrow gaps in performance among student groups across the LCFF priorities.

LEVEL 2
DIFFERENTIATED ASSISTANCE
County superintendents, the California Department of Education, and the California Collaborative for Educational Excellence provide differentiated assistance by working with school districts to address identified performance gaps among student groups.

LEVEL 3
INTENSIVE INTERVENTION
The superintendent of public instruction may require more intensive supports for local education agencies (LEAs) and/or schools with persistent performance issues and a lack of improvement over a specified time period.

RESOURCE LEADS AND INITIATIVES
run by county offices

Community Engagement

Math Initiative

Equity Lead

MTSS/SUMS
Scale up Multi-Tiered System of Support

Geographic Lead Agency
Specific County Offices of Education will be tasked with supporting other COEs in their region — helping to coordinate and bring in other supports

SELPA Resource Lead
Special Education Local Plan Areas

County Office of Education (COE)
The COE is the primary support for the district and is involved in or at least aware of all supports being provided to the district

Regional EL Specialists
English Learners

Local Education Agency (LEA)
School districts and charters

CALIFORNIA EDUCATION AGENCIES

CCEE
California Collaborative for Educational Excellence

CDE
California Department of Education

Source: California Department of Education, 2018, California System of Support

data from the dashboard) compared to how they might have performed given their demographics. Very small districts (with fewer than 200 African American or Hispanic students and fewer than 200 white students) were excluded from the analysis. This report found that 156 out of 435 districts "beat the odds" by performing better than they were expected to (Podolsky, Darling-Hammond, Doss, & Reardon, 2019). A companion in-depth study of seven positive outlier districts found that these districts had greater focus, recruited teachers with good qualifications, leveraged the new standards and assessments, and developed better pedagogy (Burns, et al., 2019).

Several other studies show that improvement in student achievement has been on the move in the last few years. Moreover, new governor Gavin Newsom, who followed Jerry Brown's eight-year term in January 2019, is supporting and significantly increasing the funding of the California Way with his "cradle to the grave" commitments from early childhood onward. Our latest report was timed to mark the turnover from Brown to Newsom and contains six major recommendations (Figure 5.5).

Figure 5.5 Six Recommendations: California

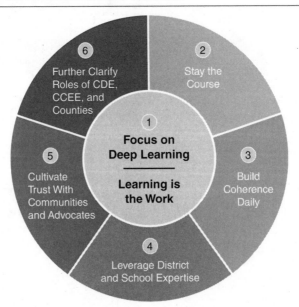

Source: Fullan, Rincón-Gallardo, & Gallagher, 2019

It is impressive that California has been able to move forward and upward in six short years given the size and complexity of the system. But there are still huge problems: Inequity is massive; the so called "advocates"—the equity crowd—are becoming more and more vociferous about the slowness of the reform; the gains are relatively modest and affect only a few of the higher order skills needed for 21st century learning; and the changes that are required strike at the center of school and district cultures—the most difficult and important aspect of achieving lasting success. It is for the latter reason that we highlighted our Recommendation 1: "Focus on deep learning: Learning is the work." This is where the details lie. Get these right and many other positive factors follow.

California has determinedly started down the pathway of capacity building, beginning to get good results on some of the basics, and liberating and equipping the middle to play a greater enabling role for local reform. The middle for California is exceedingly complex: districts, counties, support agencies like CCEE and more. And the system is yet to enter on any scale the deep learning arena.

Recall that in this chapter we are focusing on the macro level—policy makers, their staff, and agencies. Again, this is more complicated in California than almost anywhere else. There is a governor and a state superintendent of public instruction, both elected. There is the 11-member State Board of Education and the California Department of Education (which has been decimated over the years through budget cuts). This center must help bridge the connection between the culture of government and the culture of the school system; its role is to ensure communications and understanding about the joint work of improvement so that it moves back and forth between the two cultures in productive ways. Ultimately, they must use the processes within both systems to accomplish the reforms.

A word here about bridging the cultural differences between state departments of education and the school systems. Developing mutual trust and respect across the cultural divide is a crucial factor to success. In our model, trust-building is essential and governments can do something about that—by investing in the system, by participating as learners, by having good policies informed by evidence, by respecting degrees of autonomy relative to the other two levels, by enabling success and celebrating it when it occurs, and by having high expectations for all. As stated earlier, government understands it can (try to) achieve results through the use of legislation, regulation, policy, program, and incentives (usually fiscal). Educators on the other hand are motivated by the more intrinsic senses of purpose, autonomy, mastery, and connectedness. Thus, a fundamental misunderstanding between the school system and government is that staff in schools (the people on whom successful changes for students ultimately depend) don't care much about the policy levers around which the work of government revolves. School staff will comply with minimum legal standards, will align with programs that make sense to them, and will try to take advantage of any resources available to do what they already know is good for their students. What sometimes looks like resistance on their part may actually be practical survival, governments and priorities change far more quickly than students move through the school system, and educators feel they know their students and schools and what is best better than those more distant. Educators may also appear to resist acting on a change because they don't understand what to do to effect the change. Both sides of the divide can inadvertently be arrogant about their own wisdom and critical of the ineptitude of the other.

For a reform to succeed, it must build momentum over time. Governments will need to move away from a compliance mindset to a more responsive stance, working with the middle to develop solutions to implementation challenges as they arise. Staff in schools will need to have growing confidence in the reforms and increasingly take on the leadership and implementation of the changes across the system. Local educators will need to know that their views are valued by government; and this takes nurturing of respectful relationships and modeling of decision-making based on research and evidence. Above all else, the State Department or Ministry of Education will need to have a collaborative mindset, building teams with other groups within the Department of Education, and partnering with groups across the school system to build coherence in the broader work of the department with counties, districts, and schools. The reform process and its implementation must become the core work of the school system. To the degree possible, the rest of the work of the Department should either be coherent with the reforms underway or at the very least be led with minimum distractions to the schools.

Reform needs to be increasingly owned and led by the middle and locals in the field. Co-leadership between the center and other levels must be carefully developed and monitored. It begins with early recognition that there are already a number of schools and districts who can lead components of the work, engaging them in narrating, modeling, and networking what they do to improve student and staff learning. It continues as the government begins to provide differentiated work with schools. Some activities and expectations will involve all schools and districts working together to learn and implement changes. Some schools and districts will very quickly demonstrate they know how to improve their impact on student learning and can articulate their journey. These can become allies to building the cultural changes needed at other schools who are earlier in the transition. Most schools or districts will need assistance in some components of leading improvement in their areas, and their needs can inform the learning that networks at various levels can take on. And a few schools will struggle deeply and will need ongoing partnering and assistance and sometimes direct help, making it all the more important that the "system" has mechanisms in place to identify and team with others who can provide support at the early stages of development.

> The State Department or Ministry of Education will need to have a collaborative mindset, partnering with groups across the school system to build coherence in the broader work of the department with the schools.

Finally, we would say that guidelines or related documents often come to districts as checklists or statements of key issues components that need to be addressed such as developing instructional leadership, selecting high yield strategies, and so on. Rarely do these lists approach the problem from a "systems perspective." Moreover, we remind the reader that a checklist is only as good as the mindset using it. Even the right elements require linkage ideas or networking, which would be essential to implementing the components. As we have stated frequently, progress is almost always a matter of establishing ongoing *social processes* that are focused, specific, and linked to learning outcomes (goodness is in the details as we saw in the positive outlier districts).

BEWARE OF (SEDUCTIVE) DISTRACTORS

We have one more "strange attractor" (to use language from chaos theory) that appears in cases like California where there is great need, widespread government support, and willingness to spend money. Such a period last existed in the 1970s in which we found a widespread reform effort on the part of governments in the United States. We used to refer to it as the "tyranny of opportunity" (which for now we can define as too many ad hoc initiatives, each accompanied by money). Indulge us while we set up the argument. A landmark study of education system change in the 1970s became known as the *Rand Change Agent Study* (Berman & McLaughlin, 1977; Fullan, 1982). Here we see two factors at work that today we would call a perfect storm. On the one hand, governments in power in buoyant times (political majority and a willingness to spend money) pass many new policies or program initiatives—they have an adoption mentality (not worrying as much about implementation). The adoption bias is the tendency to get the policy "on the books." Satisfaction derives from the passage of the legislation.

On the other hand, the recipients of the money—districts and schools—can have what the Rand researchers call an "opportunistic" or "problem-solving" orientation to the resources. Opportunistic is "give us the money." Problem solving is "we know our problems and will only take the money if it meets our needs." The perfect storm of course is lots of ad hoc adoptions combined with indiscriminate consumers.

Returning to California as a case example, recall that we have enormous structural complexity: governor and legislature, state board, state superintendent, Department of Education, counties, districts, and a new semiautonomous support agency called the California Collaborative for Educational Excellence (CCEE). Most of these entities have new role descriptions (and many new people). What to do? We take as a case example El Dorado County, which is one of the 58 counties in the state—one we have a close working relationship with (see Vignette 5.3).

VIGNETTE 5.3
Leadership From the County

El Dorado County

El Dorado County Office of Education (EDCOE), in California near the border of the state of Nevada, is one of 58 counties. It consists of 15 mostly rural districts with some 28,000 students. We have worked with the county for the past two years at its invitation because it wanted to increase its system effectiveness according to the ideas we have been finding and developing. The county superintendent is Ed Manansala, who also happens to be the president of the California County Superintendents Educational Services Association (CCSESA), representing all 58 counties. As we presented ideas to the group of EDCOE leaders and the 15 superintendents, we focused on the need for the middle (i.e., them) to develop an approach where they could control the agenda in the context of system reform. We asked Manansala to provide a brief account of how El Dorado County and its districts were proceeding with the reform. To us, this represents one concrete example of the kind of thinking and action at the middle that we have in mind, recognizing that the 58 counties reflect a wide range of sizes and local conditions. El Dorado County is, in fact, one of the smaller counties. Here is Manansala's response:

> In April 2019, at the Superintendents' retreat in South Lake Tahoe, the leaders representing the 15 districts in El Dorado County made a declaration, "We will relentlessly focus on teaching and learning in El Dorado County."

**Why Did the Superintendents
Choose to Focus on Teaching and Learning?**

> I have been leading for over 30 years. I have never felt the struggle of making sense of all this work like I have this past year. (Dr. Jim Tarwater, Superintendent of Lake Tahoe Unified)

(Continued)

(Continued)

Prior to the unified declaration, the superintendents were reflecting on the overwhelming and exponentially growing number of demands unfolding on districts over the last six years. Dr. Jim Tarwater's experience in the Lake Tahoe Unified School District (LTUSD) captured the essence of the struggle. Since the implementation of the Local Control Funding Formula in 2013, the demands in LTUSD have progressively grown. The factors are reflected in the following activities (read, requirements) that occurred in LTUSD in one academic year:

- The Local Control Accountability Plan process
- Qualification for Differentiated Assistance
- Special Education Performance Indicator Review (PIR)
- Comprehensive Support and Improvement review (under Every Student Succeeds Act)
- Western Association of Schools and Colleges review (WASC)

The Problem: Distraction and Clutter

Many aspects of the California educational reforms are embraced by the district superintendents. Specific reforms embraced are higher standards for student learning, a multiple-measured accountability system, increased resources for districts with a focus on local control and equity, and a partnership approach with the El Dorado County Office of Education (rather than punitive accountability). While the elements and focus are welcomed, the intense rollout of the reforms has unintentionally created a sense of distraction and clutter to the core work: teaching and learning.

The Ask and the Challenge

During the superintendents' retreat, an emerging theme became prevalent. With the goal to focus on teaching and learning and in the context of multiple reform initiatives, the strong desire for coherence was evident. How can El Dorado County achieve a framework and practice that provides coherence and focuses on teaching and learning?

EDC's Solution/Theory of Action: A Developing Framework to Focus on Teaching and Learning

El Dorado Professional Improvement Community (EPIC)

Districts will be given the opportunity to build professional capacity while working with El Dorado County colleagues, experts in the field, and high-quality data tools to implement change ideas leading to improvement around the California Dashboard measures. Trained staff will provide a structured review of Dashboard data, local data, and predictive data from CORE.

Teams, including site leaders, district leaders, district data specialists, teacher leaders, specialists for special education, EL (English Learners), and foster youth, will use data to inform and identify an area of focus for the year. Through four facilitated learning sessions, districts will also have the opportunity to weave together various accountability requirements: Differentiated Assistance (Dashboard), ESSA [Every Student Succeeds Act], and Performance Indicator Review (PIR). EDCOE staff will provide support to teams throughout the school year and between learning sessions (Ed Manansala, personal communication, September 20, 2019).

There is more to the strategy than this, and EDCOE is still at the early stages, but one can see the kind of initiative that is required in order to maintain a relentless focus on instructional practice when you are operating in a labyrinth of well-intentioned and supportive system reform.

As we noted, El Dorado is only one of 58 counties and one of the smaller ones at that. The county offices historically have played primarily a compliance role relative to districts concerning federal and state requirements. Imagine the challenge now as they are expected to play a supportive role. This is the bigger job of the CCSESA (the association of county superintendents). The good news is the counties by and large are committed to changing from compliance to capacity building. The bad news is that they don't know how to do it and many districts are not sure they want them to do it. Such is life in the middle in California, and we hope the reader can see that the job of sorting this out is not one for the top alone, but one that requires all three (actually four) levels: state, county, districts, and schools and community. Details, details, details!

Recall that we said when you get a political will and lots of money being generated, it is almost guaranteed that many ad hoc opportunities will come your way (you just won't know when). What would you do, for example, if you were a county or district leader and received the following press release on June 28, 2019? The press release offered $38 million from the state for the Education Workforce Investment Grant (EWIG) related to four strands: English Learner Roadmap Policy Implementation, Special Education-Related Professional Learning, Socio Emotional Learning Positive School Climate, Restorative Justice, Computer Science, and Ethnic Studies. Without knowing what might be coming next, we can guarantee that the next four years will be flooded with "opportunities" like these.

In our system model the answer is twofold. First, whatever position you hold among the three levels, become preoccupied with the problem of coherence and focus: Treat coherence-making and focus as an endemic, never-ending challenge. Second, work on your patch of the system in whatever way you can. At the top, examine how specific proposed policies fit into the overall plan and the stage of implementation. In the middle, be a coherence-maker vis-à-vis how you work with local schools and districts. If you are local, develop a focus and use it to screen opportunities, including refusing the money if the idea does not fit your needs at a particular moment in time.

Realize that we are talking about what happens in seemingly good examples of large-scale system change. We believe that such systems will be inclined to self-correct. Ontario took many steps to tighten the focus and reduce distractors. California too is staying the course with its strong core strategy and constantly seeks feedback from practice and research as to how it can strengthen its pathway to continuous improvement. Innovation is called for and must be pursued in these and all systems. It requires constant attention because new elements of the strategy are happening all the time. And, above all, it needs to be part of an overall plan in pursuit of excellence, equity, and well-being. In short, wherever you are located, take a system perspective by considering where you fit in the overall scheme and leverage your actions accordingly.

In the meantime, there is no question in our minds that the policies and strategies employed by Ontario (2003 until mid-2018) and by California (2013–the present) have increased the trust between the field and the governments, and that educators are by and large satisfied with the nature and direction of the policies. Both Ontario and California have demonstrated success in some, but not yet all of their goals. You cannot obtain this degree of satisfaction without experiencing success—a sense of fulfillment with your work and a positive impact on students' lives and learning. Under such circumstances the center, the middle, and local levels need focus, but they also must exercise degrees of freedom, thereby improving the whole system. Both Ontario and California have come a long way and, alas, have a long way to go.

We have one more stop—Victoria, Australia.

Victoria

Victoria is the second largest in population of the six states and territories in Australia with a population of 6.5 million people. As with all states, the federal and state governments provide funds for three education sectors—independent schools, Catholic schools, and the focus of our attention, government schools (what we would call public schools). There are some 1,600 government schools headed by a Department of Education and Training (DET) with the state divided into four geographic regions. The central department is headed by the secretary (appointed by the minister of education), four regional offices, and staff that develop and disseminate policy, attend to operational and administrative needs, support implementation, and respond to local issues.

First, we offer our own interpretation as a snapshot of political history since 2002 as this does shape the culture for change. Two parties have contended for power: Labor on the left and Liberal (conservatives) on the right. Elections occur every fourth year, and the recent historical profile has had an impact on Victoria's improvement journey.

- 2002–2010: Labor government. Ontario and Victoria commenced their system reform strategy at approximately the same time.

Ontario's was specific and more precisely focused on change in the classroom; Victoria's was broadly strong but not grounded in detail.

- 2010–2014: Conservative government. Mostly eradicated the 2002–2010 education agenda without a specific replacement.

- 2014–2018: Labor government encore. A new focus on system improvement was launched with the banner of Victoria as "The Education State" and its ten goals. The reform was carefully constructed based upon much of the international learning base about successful reform and has been well supported with resources and staff.

- 2018: Labor re-elected with a landslide. The opportunity exists here to strengthen and implement the agenda evolving from 2014 and potentially succeed in the excellence, equity, and well-being agenda into the future.

> There is still considerable work to be done to move from the infrastructure as "something to be implemented" to a systemwide reform in which school staff own the reforms within their schools and classrooms.

The Focus of the Victoria Reform

The current reform places Victoria as the Education State pursuing excellence, equity, and well-being. The call for improved outcomes is accompanied by a set of ambitious achievable targets about the whole child. This work is supported by a number of documents and structures such as *FISO: The Framework for Improving Student Outcomes* (Victoria, 2015) and a document called *Learning Places* (Victoria, 2015). The umbrella vision is shown in Figure 5.6.

Since 2015, there have been a large number of regional consultation sessions about the frameworks and the reform around the state, along with several supportive documents: *High Impact Teaching Strategies* (Victoria, 2017), *Amplify* (Victoria, 2018), *Excellence: Creating a Learning System* (Victoria, 2019), and the FISO framework we mentioned above (Figure 5.7).

Educators at most levels of the system in Victoria feel that the system is going in the right direction, but we are focusing on the system level in

Figure 5.6 Ambitious Achievable Targets About the Whole Child

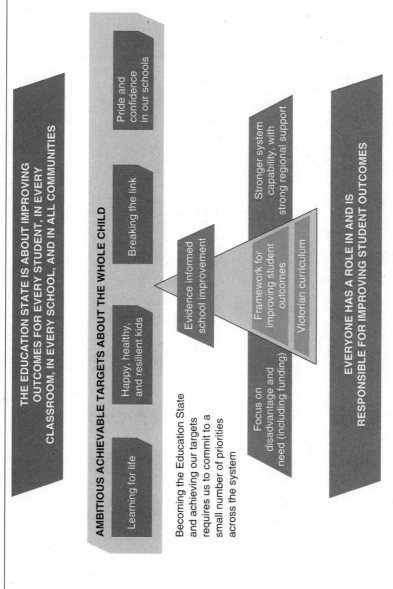

THE EDUCATION STATE IS ABOUT IMPROVING OUTCOMES FOR EVERY STUDENT, IN EVERY CLASSROOM, IN EVERY SCHOOL, AND IN ALL COMMUNITIES

AMBITIOUS ACHIEVABLE TARGETS ABOUT THE WHOLE CHILD

Learning for life

Happy, healthy, and resilient kids

Breaking the link

Pride and confidence in our schools

Becoming the Education State and achieving our targets requires us to commit to a small number of priorities across the system

Evidence informed school improvement

Focus on disadvantage and need (including funding)

Framework for improving student outcomes

Victorian curriculum

Stronger system capability, with strong regional support

EVERYONE HAS A ROLE IN AND IS RESPONSIBLE FOR IMPROVING STUDENT OUTCOMES

Source: Victoria Department of Education, 2015 (CC BY 4.0)

Figure 5.7   Framework for Improving Student Outcomes

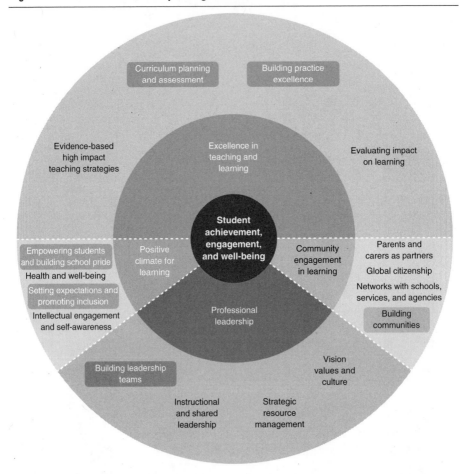

Source: Victoria Department of Education, 2015 (CC BY 4.0)

this chapter. Given our paradigm of clarity and connected autonomy at all three levels, there are a number of issues that remain to be addressed. We should like to organize these around the concept of *mindset.* Our view is that Victoria has developed a very powerful and sophisticated infrastructure to support reform, but the sense we get is that there is still considerable work to be done to move from the infrastructure as "something to be implemented" to a systemwide reform in which school staff own the reforms within their schools and classrooms. Victoria is now moving to the next phase of implementation, with broad support for the direction but seeking more concrete results. We believe that the overall plan is based upon the right drivers and theories and could be positioned along the following lines:

1. Explicitly state and cultivate schools as *partners* in the refining and implementation of the reform rather than as "recipients of a good infrastructure."

2. Related, position the plans explicitly in terms of creating a learning system (where all levels learn separately and together) rather than the language of implementation (executing a plan). This is a fine point (or to use one of our recent terms, nuanced). The documents are cast in terms of learning (e.g., *Learning Places*), but it is not always experienced as such at the local level. To say the least, this is a difficult proposition. Indeed, this is the point of our book. Change the system culture to support connected autonomy around a common learning agenda.

3. Develop a culture at the center including understanding leadership from the middle (the four regions). Many senior leaders in the Department of Education and Training are new to their positions: this provides an opportunity for new team building and coherence making within the center in relation to the regions and schools.

4. Still sticking with the center: the roles of regional offices (there are four in the state) and the support and coaching staff therein need to think through and coordinate their roles in the context of developing powerful versions of "connected autonomy" suitable to each region. This includes the relationship of the regions with the center (point 3).

Within these requirements there are certain major issues that require attention (notably these priorities are increasingly at the forefront of the agenda of strong systems of reform). They include:

1. **Equity and excellence.** How to tackle equity and excellence as integrated priorities? Sometimes people can feel that too much attention is paid to equity, thereby neglecting excellence—a false dichotomy for us, but one that can lead to unnecessary tensions between the two.

2. **Secondary school transformation.** The government has turned its attention to reform in secondary schools. Almost everywhere in the world, secondary school transformation represents unfinished business. So far, some of the issues that are arising include student agency, a broader definition of success, engaging deep and real-world learning, and a culture of innovation. Add to this: the role of exit exams, the relevance of senior curriculum, the matter of engaging pedagogy, and the role of technical education. Such a menu of secondary school reform represents new opportunities to partner with secondary schools, which we expect that the government will take up.

3. **Rural and regional reform.** How to tackle regional differences when it comes to lower achievement, aspiration and choice, recruitment and retention of staff, and engaging learning for students in rural areas? The development of education in rural areas is a worldwide issue, and Victoria is poised to tackle this domain.

Addressing these cutting-edge issues is all to the credit of Victoria leaders. In the spirit of our book, the obvious dilemmas requiring attention and resolution include the following: the "complicatedness" of overload and fragmentation when you try to do too much that is not connected; insufficient attention to the pedagogical core (the issue we highlighted in California); the capability of principals and other school leaders to lead complex change without initiative fatigue; and a potential failure to focus with enough precision and responsive attention to detail. And finally, a significant challenge also facing Victoria (and many governments) is to become preoccupied with student outcomes without backfilling the route to get there. Such a predilection can lead to poor forms of accountability when the real need is to go deep into teacher-student learning. How to get accountability right in the midst of systemwide transformation is a perennial issue for all action-oriented jurisdictions.

In any case, these issues and the work moving forward, as in our other two cases, place Victoria in the forefront of system reform and its inner dynamics. Victoria is deeply engaged in trying to figure this out and it is at the beginning of its current political term of four years that could turn into eight if the incumbents were to get re-elected in 2023.

LAYERED, CONNECTED AUTONOMY

We are back to our main premise. Governments need to conceptualize their roles differently. Systems have become too complex to run from the center. They need to provide good direction underpinned by the core values of equity, excellence, and well-being. They need to frame some of the main ways of getting there: focused collaborative practices, engaging pedagogies, deep learning for all, higher order outcomes like the 6Cs, peers and networks learning together, and nonpunitive but nonetheless explicit accountability. They need to get their act together centrally through direction, lateral learning, and cohesion at the top. They need to participate as learners with those at other levels where they offer their "expertise" in what they come to know and act as apprentices in areas where they have less knowledge. They need to harvest this group learning and produce resources and supports, which help spread successful practice and communicate both the urgency going forward and the successes to date, building a critical momentum to the work. And they need to invest resources into this agenda and the progress it brings.

The center should define its role as a partnership with the other two levels where mutual learning around a definable, ambitious agenda is the core of the strategy. Lateral and vertical learning serves up good ideas but then frames actions toward what works. Chances are that people will do the right thing because of their peers, more so than those above them, but the truth is *both* peers and the hierarchy are influential in our model in action.

This notion of a partnership can be modeled and trust can be built through transparent processes of developing and implementing key processes. Ultimately, system change is about having schools become more precise in their self-assessments and planning processes, without becoming overly prescriptive. The expectation is that eventually all schools will use good processes that in effect will become mandatory, but our advice would be to start with the mindset that it is voluntary but inevitable. The culture shift desired is that schools will adopt these practices not out of compliance but rather because they see them as processes they own, which are useful and which ultimately deliver upon the deep moral purpose of high-quality learning for all students.

As an example, in Ontario, we very much wanted to avoid the compliance mindset that inevitably results in lots of effort and no improvement. Soon after the large systemwide conferences to bring everyone to a common understanding of the goals, the Literacy and Numeracy Secretariat (LNS) began to model two beliefs: that the system at all levels had to learn to use practical research differently to inform immediate changes in the joint work, and that the ministry (or LNS in this case) was committed to gathering the research and producing practical useful documents and resources that were respectful of school workload. In the case of the development and implementation of a School Effectiveness Framework (SEF) that guided the improvement processes, we began with a gathering and release of considerable research around the factors that make schools more effective. The first document was a draft, and the LNS asked schools across the system for feedback so all schools could benefit from improvements to the resources. All districts were asked to identify at least some schools that would use the resource and be part of the research and feedback process. Early developments like these created schools and some district personnel who became local experts to assist other schools in implementation in subsequent cycles of change.

Once the feedback was received, the document was significantly streamlined (processes and plans need to be as straightforward as possible so that schools can spend their time changing teaching and learning, not just planning for it). Plans were expected to be concise with no more than three or four action targets and with a total plan of ideally fewer than five pages. The School Effectiveness Framework was then refined and released in draft form with a request for feedback the subsequent year. There was a process not just for school annual self-assessment but also one for an external review (by a district team of colleague, principal, and supervisor reviewers with a focus on feedback to the school regarding its plans and actions, and whether evidence could be seen in classrooms reflecting the planned changes). Districts were asked to engage all their elementary schools and some of their secondary schools in self reviews and to "try out" the external review process in some schools. It was only in the third year and in the third revised release of the document that it became an expectation that all schools engage in an annual SEF self-assessment and improvement planning process and that all districts have in place a process for an external review of every school within a five-year cycle.

In many ways the SEF was never an official requirement, but everyone ended up using it—voluntary but inevitable as we say. At the time the SEF was made a mandatory expectation, but it was never associated with a mandatory compliance provision. Districts proudly and publicly stated that they were "ahead of" provincial expectations as they had already implemented the expected cycles of improvement planning. And by then most schools and districts talked about the increasing precision they were building into their planning. This process allowed districts and schools to begin the change in their cultures to one that was more evidence based and built up a more trusted partnership between the ministry and the system. It is an excellent example of government process remaining nimble and responsive to implementation work in the field in order to engage people at the local level in leading improvement. It ends up being stronger accountability than can be obtained by any top-down system. Ironically, the top becomes more influential on the ground in this system of layered connectivity.

As the work in these processes spreads across the system, the department can build expectations by communicating the narrative increasingly clearly: that all schools are engaged in improving student learning and well-being; and that the best worldwide research and evidence about improvement, including the work of successful practitioners in the state, form the basis for action. Thus, the emphasis becomes one of improvement and implementation, accompanied by constant revisions to strategies in response to impact on learning. Complex plans that sit on shelves or in computers go out the window.

We see another powerful example of positioning the top differently and using the middle to leverage rapid change in our deep learning work in Uruguay, a small, poor country at the bottom of Latin America with a population of 3.5 million and some 3,500 schools. Faced with almost no technology-based learning, the government set up a new unit in 2007 called Plan Ceibal. The idea was to establish an innovative unit that would parallel the Ministry of Education, partnering with the ministry and schools to move the system forward in the use of technology for learning as quickly as possible. Working as one of our partners in npdl.org, Ceibal began deep learning with 100 schools in 2014, and rapidly expanded to 200, then 400, and now 600 schools—almost a quarter of all schools in the country. At a deep learning conference in Toronto in November 2019, the president of Ceibal, Miguel Brechner, showed that access to computers for all age groups increased dramatically from 2007 to 2017. For example, use by students in the lower two quintiles, ages 6–13, increased from 9% to 99% for the bottom quintile, and 28% to 92% for the second to last quintile. Examples of quality deep learning initiatives in action abound (see Fullan et al., 2018, and Quinn et al., 2020). Ceibal coordinated the top and leveraged the middle (networks of schools) to obtain rapid change across a whole system.

State departments can also model both curiosity about possible innovations to improve student learning and well-being as well as respect for research and evidence by commissioning independent research to assess various components and strategies, which are part of the reforms. The state departments could then share the results with the system in transparent ways and work with the system to refine the work in response to the research results and be informed by those getting early success. At a system level, this is parallel to the expectations for teachers—that they will try new strategies based on evidence, examine the impact on student learning, share with their colleagues, and refine their teaching in response.

The center can also fuel improvements to teaching and learning through the sharing of evidence to inform and accelerate the improvement cycle. Student learning, well-being, and engagement increase when teachers are able to use a variety of high-impact teaching strategies well in their classrooms and there is now a worldwide body of research that identifies much about what these successful teaching strategies are. Schools and teachers should not have to do all of this original research themselves; they should be focused on implementing the changes required. Victoria, as we mentioned earlier, addressed this problem with the publication of the document called HITS: *High Impact Teaching Strategies.* It is an excellent guide to ten strategies and the research behind them, and principals and teachers love it. Victoria supplements these with videos showing teachers' and leaders' success stories and thinking throughout the process. Ontario chose to produce high-quality videos showing what a range of good teaching strategies looked like in classrooms across the province, giving teachers voice in describing why they chose certain approaches and how their students responded. California is in the process of coming to terms with how to provide this information.

Learning, well-being, and engagement increase when students receive high quality, consistent feedback on their work and how to improve it. Yet most school systems, when they look at their data, find that teacher assessment of student work from classroom to classroom or grade to grade is often inconsistent across classrooms, and inconsistent as well with curriculum expectations and standards. Constantly changing and often arbitrary decisions about expected levels of performance can frustrate students and in the worst case undermine their sense of efficacy. If teachers and students want to see more students reach the highest levels of achievement, they need to know what excellent work at that level looks like. They need precision in what a student needs to understand and what skills they need to demonstrate in order to excel. What kind of feedback is most effective for teachers to give students, to give each other, for students to give each other, and to inspire them forward? In the midst of the reforms, Ontario released a new assessment document with a lot of attention paid to formative assessment, differentiated approaches, and the use of assessment rubrics connected to curriculum goals and pathways. The ministry provided the structures and some sample rubrics for assessment. At the local level, assessment rubrics started out being designed by teachers. They were then shared with others as the discussions that ensued were rich sources of professional learning. And soon teachers were engaging students in looking at learning goals in the curriculum and co-designing assessment rubrics for use in their classrooms. This process helped student understanding of the goals of learning become much more precise and achievable, helping them develop increased metacognition skills to apply to their own lifelong learning journey.

As schools set their improvement goals, a department of education should monitor them. If the plans are weak, materials might be developed to provide feedback on them or to share and demonstrate what particularly effective plans being used across the system look like. Increasingly, these plans should address deep learning goals as well as pathways to excellence, equity, and well-being often in integrated ways. As the reforms take shape, principals and regional leaders will need to grow in their ability to lead instructional improvement. This is a key area in which state departments of education can partner with principals and regional leaders and with their professional associations, providing leadership development programs, courses, mentoring, and networks. We have commented in earlier chapters on regional and principal leadership as we explored the work at those levels of the system.

Obviously, for all of this work to happen, both within the government and in the schools, there must be a significant allocation of funds. Effective systems learn to put the money on strategies that have impact. With respect to a school system that is open to learning, the return on the investment is great: increased learning outcomes including greater equity, stronger student well-being and engagement, and staff with a growing sense of professional efficacy and subsequent willingness to take on new challenges.

In each year, a government provides a large investment into its education system, often the second largest ministry within government. The vast majority of these dollars is spent in paying for the ongoing work of the education system. It has long been an observation that it is not how much money a system possesses but *how* it is spent. We cannot carry out a full financial analysis. Certainly, investing in early learning and teacher quality is essential. We do know that when it comes to developing and implementing systemwide reform, additional and dedicated funds are required. These funds are small compared to the total expenditure, but they can be substantial in their own right and can be successfully leveraged to provide resources (primarily time for school staff and regional staff to network, to lead, and to support the work), which will actually result in the desired changes taking place. In short, large funds are spent to provide the normal year-to-year components of schools and education; the relatively small additional funds for reform implementation are a necessary catalyst that produces improved results over time and pays big dividends in a community, an economy, and our planet for years to come. All of this plays itself out through what we called above "layered, connected autonomy" across and within local, middle, and top levels of the system.

CONCLUSION

Having said all this, we believe that existing systems must shift their energy and focus to deep learning in which global competencies (such as the 6Cs), radically new pedagogy consisting of partnerships and leveraging technology, and immersion in the content of *engaging the world changing the world*, form the essence of learning and acting in the rest of the 21st century (Fullan et al., 2018; Quinn et al., 2020). The top has the most difficult role of all, which is to orchestrate a system that is so complex that it is incapable of "doing what it is told." The center can, however, be enormously influential, especially if it has eight or more years in power. If it cultivates connected autonomy, it leaves a legacy of capacity building that carries over beyond its term. In Ontario, for example, there is great capacity at the school and district level that serves them well in the face of a contrary government. Indeed, in our deep learning work we are beginning to see school and district levels develop pedagogical and political power vis-à-vis the excellence, equity, and well-being agenda. In so doing, they are becoming a source of innovation for the system.

Wise governments invest in, and/or take advantage of innovation in the middle to stimulate wider system change. Political change is inevitable, and some environments are more conducive to progress than others, so we need an education system that makes substantive progress when the conditions are right and that protects the gains and leads itself forward when the conditions are less favorable. Over time such systems provide the foundation upon which long-term progress can be built.

As societal stakes become more and more serious (Part I of this book), and as students and teachers develop capacity and commitment to transform their worlds, collective learning becomes almost unstoppable. At some point we expect that the pedagogical and political pathways will converge, and all three levels come to coexist, most often for better system results; and yes, sometimes necessarily in tension. We say necessarily because disagreements along the way are inevitable, but also because constructive conflict (the kind you get in systems of connected autonomy) results in breakthroughs and progress along the way. Overall across the three levels, the issues that we have examined over the past three chapters begin to show a picture where each level can be influential in achieving system reform through its own actions and through the connected efforts with the other two levels. The end result is that the details and the big picture establish a new rapport.

Part III

The New World

There will be a new world whether we like it or not.

The current situation is too volatile. The world will either worsen into deep climatological and social terrorism where distrust and pessimism will dominate, or it will evolve as a dynamic and exciting universe with open-ended optimism. The *system* will dominate for better or worse. We are at a time in history when the formal school system has lost its way. Learning is clearly at a premium in an age of technology, creativity, threat, inequity, contact without closeness, and vulnerability for humans from cradle to grave. We may not be facing the biggest upheaval of all time, but we are facing one that greater percentages of humans of all ages are fundamentally anxious about. Moreover, there seems little doubt that in the space of two generations (some 50 years), humankind has been party to creating the biggest people-generated climatological catastrophe and social threat of extreme inequity ever encountered on earth. The world is really becoming increasingly uninhabitable.

Society, in other words, is at the crossroads. Education must choose between being a recipient of whatever society dishes up or an active agent of transformation. One way or another, education will contribute to the possibilities either as a passive recipient of a disastrous society or as the chief instrument of expanding fulfillment. For the latter to transpire, each of the three levels of the system will have to contribute magnificently in its own right and collectively as connected players in symphonic harmony. Learn what not to do from the bad examples; get insights from the good ones. Ultimately be the system you want to become. There is literally no time to spare!

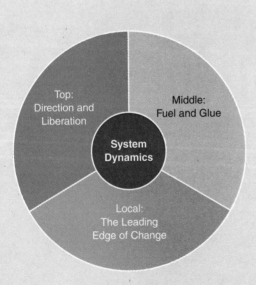

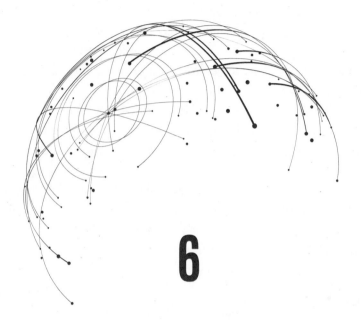

6

Where Do We
Go From Here?

The core messages of this book are: (1) cherish and foster your own connected autonomy; (2) connect to others in your vicinity; (3) be a system player in your own state, province, or country (as in connect upwards to contribute more broadly); and (4) be concerned about where the world is heading. The figure on the facing page captures the essence of our system argument. The leading edge of actual change happens at the local level. The middle, within the state framework, and in light of local knowledge and partnership, responds to local needs and provides critical fuel and glue for focused action. The top frames and invests in core direction and interacts and liberates energy at the other levels, while monitoring and stimulating progress intervening where necessary.

In evolutionary terms we saw in Chapter 1 that people need the close bonds of an intimate group, but we also made the case that all of us need to be actively concerned about the universe. Be close at home and engaged at large because the future depends on us—the majority of us working in a problem-solving, creative manner. Cataclysmic destruction or creative genius may be the binary choice. We all have a responsibility to tip the odds in favor of the latter.

No one government can carry the day. A student's journey through school lasts a lot longer than most governments. When we think about improving student learning, we set ourselves on a long and multiyear journey. The system stands a chance for success when the top guides and supports it in the right ways (the right drivers). But governments change and some seem unable to figure out guided leadership and multifaceted partnerships or are otherwise wedded to the wrong actions. If we are to serve students and improve education over the long term, we need to maximize the development in the good times (sailing with the wind at our backs and on a direct course), working to have it owned by the field and fueled by a sense of teacher and leader efficacy, so that when we end up in the bad times, schools and districts can keep their heads down, preserve the progress made, and continue the work. Then conditions change and the system can once again leverage itself forward. After a few iterations, the system retains and builds on the good things and learns to avoid or jettison more of the bad things. Do your part and evolution will take care of the rest. The remaining sections furnish a few more ideas and reminders about how to further nudge evolution.

DETAILS, DETAILS, DETAILS

What does the devil in the details really mean? Presumably, it means there are lots of details with many of them unknown in advance (partly because new details are generated through interaction requiring new detailed action at all three levels in response—the system must be nimble and responsive in smart ways). One way or another some of these neglected details will wound your effort, and when they interact and accumulate, it could be fatal. First, let us underscore the fact that this is not bad luck; *it is the nature of the beast.* We call this beyond complexity. This means that at a certain point of dynamism—and we have long passed this point since the turn of the century—it becomes impossible to predict in advance how the details will unfold. As Duncan Green, longstanding activist involved in improving systems in developing countries, states, "[When it comes to human systems,] because of the sheer number of relationships, and feedback loops among their many elements, they cannot be reduced to simple chains of cause and effect" (Green, 2016, p.10).

Heifetz and Linsky (2017) draw a similar conclusion about complex adaptive change:

> For transformation change to be sustainable, it not only has to take root in its own culture, but also has to successfully engage its changing environment. It must be adaptive to both internal and external realties. (p. xiv)

In these contexts, systems thinking changes everything. It says solutions are unknown in advance. Green warns against dumbing down complex situations to simple solutions: "Such narratives squeeze out the more nuanced views of local people, and the deeper underlying causes of conflict, and end up promoting superficial victories rather than real change" (2016, p. 223).

As the apocryphal story about the economics professor goes, when faced with a successful example that did not fit his theory (it is almost always a him), he noted, "That's all well and good, but will it work in theory?"

One other advance warning for our worry list comes from Mary Parker Follett, the pioneer leadership management expert from the 1920s whom we talked about earlier. We praised her advice about striving for unity of purpose with the group. But then to disabuse us that this is a one-stop, front-end task, Follett added, "But don't expect it to last for more than 15 seconds!" Dynamism indeed.

Our book really is a critique of typical approaches to system change (top down, hyperrational, chaotic) and (we hope) a clear, powerful alternative to address the very same goal: how to change systems. Our fundamental frame is to consider each of the three levels of local, middle, and macro as *equally* semiautonomous—a phenomenon we call "universal connected autonomy." The two key messages are, on the one hand, consider yourself autonomous from the other two levels, and on the other hand, make sure you "connect"—ideally as proactive consumers with the other levels (exploit upward), partnering downward (liberating individuals and especially groups), learning from others within your level (lateralize learning), and seeking two-way communication with the other levels (vertical learning).

As we said at the outset, our book delves into the truth about the devil and the details as system change is attempted. Hypothetically, two systems can each develop all of the right foundational components—improvement plans, goals, literacy, deep learning strategies, professional development for educators, and relationships of trust—but one system gets results and sustainable improvements in student learning and ability to take on the world, while the other, actually most, do not. It is in the details that the difference is made. It is found in the ways in which trust is built and students, staff, and communities are engaged. It is found within the ways in which reforms remain nimble and flexible in response to what is happening in the field. Success resides in both the content and tone of the communications from leaders, communications that must be ubiquitous, up, down and laterally on a continuous basis, inspiring people to do the work, engaging them in evidence-informed actions designed to address the deep moral purpose of our students and our own futures.

> Our fundamental frame is to consider each of the three levels of local, middle, and macro as *equally* semiautonomous—a phenomenon we call "universal connected autonomy."

The good news is that leaders can learn how to recognize details that matter—a capacity that includes being sensitive to the emergence of patterns that portend failure or success. The big, cut-across solution comes from our study of *nuance* (Fullan, 2019). Effective leaders, at all levels, are experts in *understanding context*. Context is where the details reside. Now we can make the transition from the devil, not to god, but to heaven (a more communal term).

SYSTEM CHANGE

The work at the macro and middle levels proceeds in relatively close parallel. The leadership moves required at a provincial or state level have more to do with policy, program, and funding, as well as working, leading, and learning with the middle. In Chapter 4 we used Figure 4.2 to outline the things that successful districts or regions do to effect system improvement. These activities don't exist in a vacuum; they are necessary activities for regions to take whether or not they are supported or initiated by a state or province. But in systems that have the benefit of tri-level coherence, many of the activities of a successful district are built upon the foundations of strong strategic leadership at the state level. Figure 6.1 illustrates this point in which state-district partnerships help develop the capacity for system success.

Figure 6.1   Successful District-Government Relationships

Successful Districts	Government Leadership
Jointly determine focus on learning	Establish goals for the reform.
Build coherence	Establish goals; create planning tools for the system.
	Build data and monitoring systems.
	Implement initiatives that support and align with the reform goals.
Build collaborative cultures as they recruit and build professional capital	Create resource and support networks and capacity building for school and district leaders:
	• For school and district improvement planning
	• For staff capacity building and support
	Develop and provide resources to address system challenges.
	Engage stakeholder groups (unions, principal associations, trustees, parent and community groups) in supporting the reforms and developing resources.
Differentiate support	Monitor and respond to the implementation and impact of reform activities.
	Develop and implement programs of differentiated support to districts and schools.
Communicate and influence	Use goal setting, resourcing, differentiation, and support as ongoing opportunities for communications, mobilization, and influence.
Engage in inquiry	Engage and complete research and evaluation of the major program components of reform.

Our theory of action that stimulates system learning leverages degrees of autonomy along with the vertical and lateral interactions that fuel focus and mutual learning (Figure 6.2).

A number of other ideas follow. First, theories of change (why things are the way they are and what might need to be different) must encompass what people at each of the three levels think. Notes David Green, "rarely it seems do experts show interest in poor people's own theories of change" (2016, p. 237). Further, if it is so essential to expect the unexpected, why not put yourself in a position where you are more likely to notice new developments. You can do this by "putting good feedback and response systems in place" (Green, 2016, p. 240), and by "[starting] with listening and learning, finding out where people are, valuing what is best in what people already know value and do, and [building] from there" (Heifetz & Linsky, 2017, p. xiv).

Second, participate as a learner in all your interactions. Martin and Osberg (2017) put it best: "Be an expert and an apprentice." In other words, don't shy away from contributing what you (think) you know (but don't start with this), and be prepared to learn from others, especially those in different circumstances (students, community members, the homeless). Related to this is what we think is an absolutely riveting insight from our colleague Brendan Spillane: "Every time you go to a new context you become by definition automatically *de-skilled*" (cited in Fullan, 2019). You bring expertise to the new situation, but you also likely have a lot to learn, and you use both to propel change. This is why we so often find that the most effective leaders, in addition to having a strong moral purpose, combine humility, high expectations, commitment to situational learning, and perseverance.

Figure 6.2   System Action in a Nutshell

1. Theories of change must encompass what people at each level (local, middle, macro) think.

2. Participate as a learner in all interactions. Be humble enough to know that you have a lot to learn from those you manage and supervise, from your colleagues, and from your superiors in the system.

3. Networking and collaboration are key to success.

Third, we are finding out that even the best lists of key factors are, well, just lists! Lists never scale—culture does. Thus, networking and collaboration are key to success (at every level, seeking the wisdom of the crowd), but the discussion must also be informed by evidence and is enhanced as well through the occasional presence of a knowledgeable other (this guards against groupthink). It is a culture shift within the system at all three levels. Culture shifts are about people and their views and thinking, so leading such a change requires thoughtful action and support both for the tasks and for human development and engagement along the way. What makes lists coalesce is focused and specific collaboration— evidence and experientially informed, with an accompanying predilection for action and curiosity about impact and potential improvement.

Summing up, details, especially surprising ones arising from interactions, are inevitable. People who do best are ones who participate as learners, selectively absorbing and tending to particulars that matter for better or worse. Also, and crucially, nuanced leaders foster such learning stances with all those they work with, having many collective opportunities to process the details as they work and act together. The end result is that directly and indirectly the system is much more likely to know and act on what is being learned day after day. To borrow one of Pasi Sahlberg's favorite songs, they are always "Knockin' on Heaven's Door."

THE GLOBAL SOUTH AND THE GLOBAL NORTH

It is beyond the scope of our book to analyze the worldwide system of education. But we do want to make some obvious connections in terms of how the global agenda of education development seems to be evolving with the good news that there are increasing points of communality, lessons to learn from each other, and the need to respect the unique stage of development in each country.

In the last few years there is increasing (and debatable) use at the macro global level of the terms *Global South* and *Global North*. These terms are approximately, but not in all cases, based on geography— categorized also by development and wealth. We use the terms mainly for general ease of reference. The South typically includes Africa, large parts of Asia (except Japan, Singapore, and South Korea), South America, and the Caribbean. The North refers to mainly Western countries, including Australia, New Zealand, and the more developed Asian countries mentioned above. Our comments in this section are not dependent on a precise categorization. Essentially, the book so far has been based on the Global North. Here we extend the discussion to include a comparison to the so-called Global South.

Oplatka (2019) provides a review of reform efforts in developing countries (the Global South) and draws the following points. First, he stresses that reform efforts in developing countries are based on what he calls "neo-liberalism" (a term we don't use because of its abstractness). He claims that these theories coming from the West based on top-down standardization, efficiency, narrow measurement, and punitive accountability are not suitable for developing countries. These are what we called earlier "wrong drivers," Sahlberg's GERM theory, Hargreaves and Shirley's "Third way," and so on. Moreover, our whole book makes the case that these policies do not work in the Global North either! Not only are they inappropriate for developing countries, they are outdated in the developed world.

Let's then stick with the Global South. In addition to lack of fit with Western models, the Global South has other problems: lack of capacity, poverty, limited resources, war-torn conflict, gender and race inequality, overpopulation, authoritarian and corrupt governments, and more. We agree with Oplatka that the history of external solutions from the West has been a massive failure due to superficial solutions that fail to fit local contexts, but this is now not the main point. Very recently there have been some countervailing trends that may hold some promise, including the idea that maybe the North has things to learn from the South. We turn briefly to these developments now.

There are two characteristics in the Global South that have great promise for system reform in those systems and potentially contain some lessons for the Global North. The first concerns the key role of local community and the second the combination of innovation and the mobilization of youth. Relative to the former, it is the case, as Oplatka describes it, that *communitarianism* is historically associated with self-serving authority. He summarizes some of the shortcomings this way: "Some of the criticisms concerned the blurred distinctions between the political and the civil, the absence of minorities . . . the anti-egalitarianism underlying major communitarian thoughts, and the difficulty to reconcile liberal and communitarian ideas" (2019, p. 69).

On the other hand, many local and indigenous values and cultures are in fact compatible with the moral purpose and values associated with the 6Cs and deep learning that is in the forefront of new developments in educational transformation. Buttressing all of this in the south (and increasingly worldwide) is the dissatisfaction of youth and the potential mobilization of young people as a compelling force to "engage the world change the world" (Fullan, Quinn, & McEachen, 2018). This takes us into the realm of innovation where the combination of lack of resources, need for rapid change, and the press for reform from youth and other elements create conditions conducive to novel and potentially powerful new ways for achieving transformation over shorter periods of time than we imagined possible.

Our team member Santiago Rincón-Gallardo (2019) takes us well down the new pathway of learning from the South in his aptly titled book, *Liberating Learning: Educational Change as Social Movement.* Santiago's core argument is about:

> Fundamentally changing how teachers and student interact with each other in the presence of knowledge, how educators and leaders interact with and transform their institutional surroundings to consolidate and sustain powerful learning in classrooms, and how policy and practice interact with and influence each other. (p. 15)

Such transformation of the pedagogical core also includes "disruption of social relations of power, authority, and control" as well as "establishing new social relations" (p. 54). For this work to develop and spread, argues Santiago, is not a matter of scaling but more akin to social movements for which he cites Marshall Ganz (2010). Social movements are collective agents of cultural and political transformation: [They] emerge as a result of the efforts of purposeful actors (individuals, organizations) to assert new public values, form new relationships rooted in those values, and mobilize the political, economic, and cultural power to translate these values into action (Ganz, 2010, p. 1).

Ganz identifies intrinsic motivation, salient knowledge, and continuous improvement as three core features of social movements. The strength of movements is that they mobilize and integrate social, pedagogical, and political forces where clearly the local or bottom level is empowered with connected autonomy as they develop laterally, and upward to the middle, and policy levels. In the course of this phenomenon, community engagement and grassroots innovation are greatly strengthened.

One more source of strength can be found at the macro level concerning UNESCO's multidecades work on "Developing inclusive and equitable education systems," which advocates education for all, especially those who have been left out or are otherwise disadvantaged. Such system-level strategies have made good, but not sufficient overall impact over the past 25 or so years. The question now is whether the conditions for multilevel impact are more favorable in 2020 than they have been since the late 1990s with respect to "Developing inclusive and equitable education systems." The UNESCO report recommends six action steps:

1. Establish clear definitions of what is meant by inclusion and equity in education.

2. Use evidence to identify contextual barriers to the participation and progress of learners.

3. Ensure that teachers are supported in promoting inclusion and equity.

4. Design the curriculum and assessment procedures with all learners in mind.

5. Structure and manage education systems in ways that will engage all learners.

6. Involve communities in the development and implementation of policies for promoting inclusion and equity in education. (UNESCO, 2019)

Three things strike us about this agenda. First, it is compatible with what we have advocated throughout the book. Second, although in several places the UNESCO report notes that its recommendations are intended for *all students* not just those who are underserved, the tendency is to think only of equity and inclusion, which unwittingly divert attention away from the whole system. We think this is a mistake because the fate of equity and excellence for all, in our view, is inextricably bound. To focus on inequity as a goal in itself is understandable, but misses the system point that everything must improve or nothing will as we saw with Wilkinson and Pickett's (2019) analysis of health and well-being across whole societies.

The good news, as we take up in the final section, is that conditions for new approaches to problems are more favorable and more urgent today than at any time in the past 25 years. One of these propitious conditions is that the desire for change and the types of strategies in both the Global North and the Global South have certain things in common: joint mobilization (people with the problem have to be part of determining the solution), focused learning in small collaboratives, new pedagogies, students as agents of change, parent and community participation, assessment of progress as feedback, and a nonpunitive orientation to accountability. The point: both the North and the South are actively engaged in system reform from different starting points, but once started down the pathway of transformation they may have more in common and more to learn from each other than we had hitherto realized.

> The fate of equity and excellence for all is inextricably bound.

A NECESSARY CONVERGENCE

There are many things we have not addressed in this book—the incredible complexity of global politics; the question of whether equity can ever be embraced by those who are benefiting from the present system; the potential for business and education to converge around the value of the global competencies; and the role of education as an agent of change for society, indeed for the universe.

We live in an increasingly troubled and scary world, which should alarm everyone. At the same time, there is a magnificence about the human species, its creative accomplishments, and its awesome capabilities. We have not yet figured out how best to relate to the universe or to each other. We wrote this book not just because of the dangers, but we also thought that the potential for snapping out of the awful trajectory that we are in the midst of could be transcended and that humans, individually and collectively, would want to do so—not just to avoid catastrophe, but because they are drawn to the unlimited, mysterious, and unknown future that is in many ways moving toward us.

We sense a nervous and inchoate rumbling at each of the three levels that to some extent is independent of each other but will inevitably feed on each other for better or worse. The top thankfully is expressing some doubt about its traditional ways. Sahlberg's GERMS are weakening, the "wrong drivers" are veering, and positive replacements are emerging. We saw such in California, Victoria, and Ontario until 2018 (and soon to return we predict). There are several other similar positive examples; we cited only the ones we are working closely with.

The bottom is also rumbling not just because it has been on the receiving end of bad policy and galloping inequity but also because it senses its creative potential to be agents of making a better world. And the middle is seeing that it may be ideally positioned to broker, indeed to lead brand new solutions. The combination of the autonomy and coordination of the three levels in action is our *necessary convergence*. We called it "universal connected autonomy." It is incredibly complex and so dynamic and sophisticated we may need evolution to help. But, after all, it is humans that evolve: genes, culture, and consciousness interplaying in a way that (to adapt Marshall McLuhan) shape us and then we shape them. Ping-pong without a table.

Okay, we are getting carried away, but it is kind of like what we just described. Then we add two powerful steering forces: the moral imperative of raising the bar and closing the gap (getting better at learning and better at life for everyone), and system thinking (learning to appreciate, work with, learn from, and influence "complex adaptive forces"). Our chapters in Part II attempted to show why and how each level could make an independent contribution to the whole, and to learn from the whole, and to make progress—all in processes of dynamic interaction. A fundamental part of the shift is giving education a new role away from being on the receiving end of a bad society to becoming an agent for developing a better one. Education and schools in the forefront of global development is a giant ask, but it is also enormously exciting. If not human and social education to the rescue, what or whom? The challenge is daunting and certainly represents a massive shift in the culture of an institution that has become somewhat stuck over the past 150 years. No other institution is capable of playing this role—not religion, not family, not a charismatic leader. Education should want this new role, and we should want education to want it.

System improvement requires action in the classroom and beyond in the work that teachers do with students—not just learning about, or talking about, but taking thoughtful and precise action, changing what we do as teachers, observing, monitoring, and measuring the impact of our change, and then refining, and so on as appropriate. In the words of Andy Warhol: "They always say that time changes things, but you actually have to change them yourself." Changing things with multiple, diverse individuals and groups is the challenge.

We hope our various formulations and examples provide insights and substance about *how* to develop and enable a learning culture. A big part of this involves shifting details from the devil's domain to the human realm. You do this by having many leaders with a new and more fundamental normative imperative "participate as learners" and developing others as such. These nuance leaders get below the surface and learn from and help shape details. They become experts of *context*.

The focus within context is especially on *promising pedagogy* (or learning relationships), and how learning evolves within *efficacious collaborative cultures* within the organization and across networks and other components of the system. It also involves *students as agents of change, parent and community engagement, use of evidence to inform action, and careful relations upward and outward to the system. It involves action, engaging differently together in changing the work at the students' desks so that our students will be prepared to change the world for the better.* We have provided examples of all these in action in our recent deep learning work (Fullan et al., 2018; Quinn et al., 2020).

In the course of learning from lead practitioners of all ages, we have also identified several "sticky insights"—valuable discoveries that stay with you because they capture change ideas in memorable ways. Some of these include:

- go outside to improve inside;
- go slow to go fast;
- use the group to change the group;
- focus and act, always, on the learning;
- alignment is rational, coherence is emotional; and
- strive for precision and avoid prescription.

These represent deep insights that can be easily used superficially or glibly (nuance once again). Take the last one for example. The phrase "precision not prescription" is not well understood—the precision comes in clarity and detail about what we will change in our teaching and work, as well as how we will monitor and measure the impact of those changes so we can make further adjustments on an ongoing basis in our teaching. This is not about every teacher having to do the same thing at the same time or even with the same resources.

All of this is dynamic and requires continuous interaction and processing. There are some potential questions a group may ask themselves at the end of any meeting: What is going to change in my work next week or next month because of what we have learned here today? How can I use what we have learned to improve teaching and learning in my classroom/school/district? How will I know if that is happening?

As we take stock now, there is in our view growing clarity about what to do. We know more and more about "deep learning" that in many ways mirrors what we are saying in this book. Students as agents of change and teachers as activators engage the world change the world; deep learning is good for all, but especially good for students who are most alienated. These ideas require substantial changes in the culture of schooling, and—you guessed it—in the meantime many people go about it superficially without realizing it. In short, we are at the very beginning stage of potential transformative change where failure will have its own plummeting ugliness, or where success can capture and propel humans to magical futures. Be conscious that the future is unknown and that you, individually and collectively, can do something about it. Education as an agent of change is the best weapon you have.

Our team, in partnership with the field, continue to push for this new future. Equity and excellence together is the focus. The synergy of deep learning, engagement, and well-being is the pathway toward greater fulfillment at the individual and collective levels. Life circumstances is both a cause and an outcome or effect; our life circumstances can inhibit or enhance the chances of success, and/or our experiences can alter our life circumstances. The humanity odyssey entails continuous expansion of what is possible and worthwhile (a tough judgment call, to be sure). We need fundamental transactional changes in social and economic policy and in our collective capacity to learn, which takes us back to the devil in the details and our book as a whole.

CONCLUSION: AS HUMAN AS YOU GET

There is one word that comes close to capturing the plight and pluck of humans and that is *dignity*. Wilkinson and Pickett base their whole analysis on the principle that humans feel badly or better largely on how they are doing relative to others; and when the perceived gap is great, profound problems take root. This is partly why we have concluded that equity and excellence for all is a basic human requirement. Dignity as a phenomenon has been captured vividly by photographer and writer (and PhD in physics) Chris Arnade (2019) in his recent book, *Dignity: Seeking Respect in Back Row America.*

For three years Arnade visited, photographed, and talked to scores of poor whites, blacks, Latinx, and other ethnic Americans in destitute towns and tenements in Buffalo, New Haven, Cleveland, Selma, New York City, and more. He said he embarked on this journey to back row America because he realized "I had removed myself from the realities of the majority of Americans" (2019, p. 3). There is not a good single word that could capture what he found—destitute, downtrodden, proud? This is how he describes it:

It was three years of seeing . . . how filled with pain, injustice, ambiguity, and problems too big for any one policy to address. It was also three years of seeing how resilient people can be, how community can thrive anywhere, even amid pain and poverty. (2019, p. 7)

And,

In each of these places there is a sense of having been left behind, of being forgotten—or even worse—of being mocked or stigmatized by the members of the world who are moving on and up with the GDP. (2019, p. 44)

The issues that Arnade uncovers are way beyond what we can address in this book, but they are relevant. In his words: "While trauma and racism have long been sources of rejection, lack of education is becoming a larger source as those at the bottom of our school system are falling further behind economically and socially" (2019, p. 86). In Arnade's "places" the devil is truly in the details, and there are few good ways out. Yet there is the underlying truth: "Everyone wants to feel like a valued member of something larger than themselves" (Arnade, p. 233). Valuing dignity for all is as human as you get.

In many ways saving the world is way beyond our book but in one way not so. Among children, youth and adults of all ages, in or outside education, stress appears to be at an all time high and worsening before our very eyes. All the signs point to the likelihood that society may be reaching a breaking point. What to do?

The heart of our book is that the current education system is wrong. We have concluded that massive re-focusing of education over the next two generations will be required—education that is devoted to engaging the world to change the world with all the details of deep learning that we and others have set forth. For us, education founded on equity, excellence, and well-being is the way forward toward this end.

In the vein of "evolution is smarter than you are," it has been said that Millennials (born 1980–1995) tend to be self-centered and not clear about what they might do in life. It may be no coincidence that Gen Z youth (those born after 1995) are increasingly showing two related characteristics: something like 50% high anxiety and 50% wanting to improve the world. Both of these variables feed on each other. Anxiety has been on the increase rapidly since about 2013, according to UNESCO surveys of youth, and students of all ages express the need for change in the world and are committed to working on it if they can find a way to do so. It is almost as if evolution, without any prompting, senses the necessity to radically change course. Our book agrees with this but notes that the future could go either way; that we have to do our part, and that altering learning in fundamental ways may be our only positive evolutionary way out of the potentially fatal mess we have, however inadvertently, fashioned for ourselves.

Education is society's ultimate change agent—a role that it must now take up with full force. Dare the school to create a new social order; double dare education to influence evolution for the better!

References

Ainscow, M., Chapman, C., & Hadfield, M. (2020) *Changing education system*. Milton Park, Oxford, UK: Routledge.

Arnade, C. (2019). *Dignity: Seeking respect in back row America*. New York, NY: Sentinel.

Berman, P., McLaughlin, M., Bass, G., Pauly, E., & Zellman, G. (1997). *Federal programs supporting educational change: Vol. VII: Factors affecting implementation and continuation*. Santa Monica, CA: Rand Corporation. Retrieved from https://www.rand.org/pubs/reports/R1589z7.html.

Boaler, J. (2019). *Limitless mind*. New York, NY: Harper Collins.

Burke Harris, N. (2018). *The deepest well: Healing the long-term effects of childhood adversity*. Boston, MA: Houghton Mifflin Harcourt.

Burns, D., Darling-Hammond, L., & Scott, C. (2019). *Closing the opportunity gap: How positive outlier districts in California are pursuing equitable access to deeper learning*. Palo Alto, CA: Learning Policy Institute, Stanford University

Campbell, C., Lieberman, A., & Yashkina, A. (2015). Teachers leading educational improvements. *Leading and managing, 21*(2), 90–105.

Campbell, D., & Fullan, M. (2019). *The governance core: School boards, superintendents, and schools working together*. Thousand Oaks, CA: Corwin.

Campero, A. (2019). *Genes vs. cultures vs. consciousness: A brief story of our computational minds*. Lexington, KY: Author.

Counts, G. (1932, 1978). *Dare the school build a new social order?* Carbondale, IL: Southern Illinois University Press.

Damasio, A. (2018). *The strange order of things: Life, feeling, and the making of cultures*. New York, NY: Pantheon.

Darling-Hammond, L., & Oakes, J. (2019). *Preparing teachers for deeper learning*. Cambridge, MA: Harvard Education Press.

Datnow, A., & Park, V. (2018). *Professional collaboration with purpose.* New York, NY: Routledge.

Donohoo, J., & Katz, S. (2020). *Quality implementation.* Thousand Oaks, CA: Corwin.

Economic Policy Institute. (2019). *State of working America wages, 2018.* Washington, DC: Author.

Eubanks,V. (2017). *Automating inequality: How high-tech tools profile, police, and punish the poor.* New York, NY: St. Martin's Press.

Florida, R. (2017). *The new urban crisis: How our cities are increasing inequality, deepening segregation, and failing the middle-class—and what we can do about it.* New York, NY: Basic Books.

Fullan, M. (1982). *The meaning of educational change.* New York, NY: Teachers College Press.

Fullan, M. (1997). *What's worth fighting for in the principalship.* Toronto, ON: Elementary Teachers Federation of Ontario.

Fullan, M. (2010). *All systems go: The change imperative in whole system reform.* Thousand Oaks, CA: Corwin.

Fullan, M. (2011). Choosing the wrong drivers for whole system reform. Seminar Series 204, Melbourne, AU: Centre for Strategic Education.

Fullan, M. (2015). *Freedom to change.* San Francisco, CA: Jossey-Bass.

Fullan, M (2016). Find your own Finland. Retrieved from www.michael fullan.ca.

Fullan, M. (2019). *Nuance: Why some leaders succeed and others fail.* Thousand Oaks, CA: Corwin.

Fullan, M. (2020a). The battle of the century: Catastrophe versus evolutionary nirvana. *The Australian Educational Leader, 42*(1) 8–10.

Fullan, M. (2020b). *Leading in a culture of change* (2nd ed.) San Francisco, CA: Jossey-Bass.

Fullan, M., & Boyle, B. (2014). *Big-city school reforms: Lessons from New York, Toronto & London.* New York, NY: Teachers College Press.

Fullan, M., & Quinn, J. (2016). *Coherence: The right drivers in action for schools, districts, and systems.* Thousand Oaks, CA: Corwin.

Fullan, M., Quinn, J., & Adam, E. (2017). *The taking action guide to building coherence in schools, districts, and systems.* Thousand Oaks, CA: Corwin.

Fullan, M., Quinn, J., & McEachen, J. (2018). *Deep learning: Engage the world change the world.* Thousand Oaks, CA: Corwin.

Fullan, M., & Rincón-Gallardo, S. (2017). *California's golden opportunity—taking stock: Leadership from the middle.* Retrieved from www.michaelfulan.ca

Fullan, M., Rincón-Gallardo, S., & Gallagher, M. J. (2019). *Learning is the work.* Retrieved from www.michaelfullan.ca

Furger, R., Hernández, L., & Darling-Hammond, L. (2019). *The California way: The Golden State's quest to build an equitable and excellent education system.* Palo Alto, CA: Learning Policy Institute.

Ganz, M. (2010). Leading change: Leadership, organization and social movements. In N. Nohria & R. Khurana. (Eds)., *Handbook of leadership theory and practice* (pp. 527–568). Boston, MA: Harvard Business Press.

Giridharadas, A. (2018). *Winners take all: The elite charade of changing the world.* New York, NY: Knopf.

Green, D. (2016). *How change happens.* Oxford, UK: Oxford University Press.

Hadfield, G. (2019). *Rules for a flat world: Why humans invented law and how to reinvent it for a complex global economy.* New York, NY: Oxford University Press.

Hargreaves, A., Boyle, A., & Harris, A. (2014). *Uplifting leadership.* San Francisco, CA: Jossey-Bass.

Hargreaves, A., & Fullan, M. (2012). *Professional capital: Transforming teaching in every school.* New York, NY: Teachers College Press.

Hargreaves, A., & O'Connor, M. (2018). *Collaborative professionalism.* Thousand Oaks, CA: Corwin.

Hargreaves, A., & Shirley, D. (2009). *The fourth way.* Thousand Oaks, CA: Corwin.

Hargreaves, A., & Shirley, D. (2018). *Leading from the middle: Spreading learning well-being and identity across Ontario.* Toronto, ON: CODE Consortium.

Hargreaves, A., & Shirley, D. (2020). Leadership from the middle. *Journal of Professional Capital and Community, 5*(1).

Harris, A., & Jones, M. (2020) *System recall: Leading for excellence and equity in education.* Thousand Oaks, CA: Corwin

Heifetz, R., & Linsky, M. (2017). *Leadership on the line.* Boston, MA: Harvard Business Review Press.

Héon, F., Davis, A., Jones-Patulli, J., & Damart, S., Eds. (2017). *The essential Mary Parker Follett* (2nd ed.). Montreal, QC: Author.

Huberman, M. (1983). Recipes for busy kitchens. *Knowledge, Creation, Diffusion, Utilization, 4*(4), 478–510.

Isaacson, W. (2017). *Leonardo da Vinci.* New York, NY: Simon & Schuster.

Kirp, D. (2019). *The college dropout scandal.* New York, NY: Oxford Press.

Lewis, A., & Diamond, J. (2015). *Despite the best intentions: How racial inequality thrives in good schools.* New York, NY: Oxford University Press.

Malin, H. (2018). *Teaching for purpose: Preparing students for lives of meaning.* Cambridge, MA: Harvard Education Press.

Martin, R., & Osberg, S. (2015). *Getting beyond better.* Boston, MA: Harvard Business School Press.

Mayer, J. (2016). *Dark money: The hidden history of the billionaires behind the rise of the radical right.* New York, NY: Anchor Books.

McCombs, B. (2004). The learner-entered psychological principles: A framework for balancing academic achievement and social-emotional learning outcomes. In J. Zins, M. Bloodworth., R. Weissberg, & H. Walberg (Eds.), *Building academic success in social and emotional learning* (pp. 23–29). New York, NY: Teachers College Press.

Morieux, Y., & Tollman, P. (2014). *Six simple rules: How to manage complexity without getting complicated.* Boston, MA: Boston Consulting Group.

Nathan, L. (2017). *When grit isn't enough.* Boston, MA: Beacon Press.

National Commission on Excellence in Education. (1983). *A nation at risk.* Washington, DC: Author.

Nodine, T. (2019). *California's education systems: A sum of the moving parts.* Sacramento, CA: Sacramento State University.

O'Day, J., & Smith, M. (2019). *Opportunity for all: A framework for quality and equality in education.* Cambridge, MA: Harvard University Press.

Ontario Ministry of Education. (2012). *School effectiveness framework.* Toronto, ON: Author.

Ontario Ministry of Education. (2013). *Learning for all: A guide to effective assessment and instruction for all students, kindergarten to grade 12.* Toronto, ON: Author.

Ontario Ministry of Education. (2014). *Achieving excellence: A renewed vision for education in Ontario*. Toronto, ON: Author.

Ontario Ministry of Education. (2016). *Growing success*. Toronto, ON: Author.

Oplatka, I. (2019). *Reforming education in developing countries*. New York, NY: Routledge.

Podolsky, A., Darling-Hammond, L., Doss, C., & Reardon, S. (2019). *California's positive outliers: Districts beating the odds*. Palo Alto, CA: Learning Policy Institute.

Quinn, J., McEachen, J., Fullan, M., Garner, M., & Drummy, M. (2020). *Dive into deep learning: Tools for engagement*. Thousand Oaks, CA: Corwin.

Reardon, S. F., Doss, C., Gagné, J., Gleit, R., Johnson, A., & Sosina, V. (2018). A portrait of educational outcomes in California. Palo Alto, CA: PACE. Retrieved from http://gettingdowntofacts.com/sites/default/files/2018-09/GDTFII_Report_Reardon-Doss.pdf.

Rincón-Gallardo, S. (2019). *Liberating learning: Educational change as social movement*. New York, NY: Routledge.

Sahlberg, P. (2012). *Finnish lessons: What can the world learn from education change in Finland*. New York, NY: Teachers College Press.

Schleicher, A. (2018). *World class: How to build a 21st-century school system*. Paris: OECD.

Senge, P. (1990). *The fifth discipline*. New York, NY: Doubleday.

Siebel, T. M. (2019). *Digital transformation: Survive and thrive in an era of mass extinction*. New York, NY: Rosetta.

Toronto District School Board. (2018). *Equity policy*. Author.

Toronto District School Board. (2019). *Equity as a leadership competency*. Retrieved from https://www.tdsb.on.ca/About-Us/Equity/Equity-as-a-Leadership-Competency

Tough, P. (2019). *The years that matter the most: How college makes or breaks us*. Boston, MA: Houghton Mifflin Harcourt.

Tucker, M. (2019). *Leading high-performance school systems: Lessons from the world's best*. Alexandria, VA: ASCD.

UNESCO. (2019). *The UNESCO Salamanca statement 25 years on: Developing inclusive and equitable education system*. Paris, France: Author.

Victoria Department of Education and Training. (2015). *Learning places*. Melbourne, AU: Author.

Victoria Department of Education and Training. (2017). *High impact teaching strategies*. Melbourne, AU: Author.

Victoria Department of Education and Training. (2018). *Amplify: Empowering students through voice, agency and leadership*. Melbourne, AU: Author.

Victoria Department of Education and Training. (2018). *Deeper: From surface learning to embedded practice*. Melbourne, AU: Author.

Victoria Department of Education and Training. (2018). *Excellence: Communities of practice, creating a learning system*. Melbourne, AU: Author.

Victoria Department of Education and Training. (2019). *Excellence: Creating a learning system*. Melbourne, AU: Author.

Wallace-Wells, D. (2019). *The uninhabitable earth: Life after warming*. New York, NY: Tim Duggan Books.

Weatherly, R., & Lipsky, M. (1977). Street-level bureaucrats and institutional innovation: Implementing special education. *Harvard Educational Review*, *47*(2), 171–197.

Wells, R. (2019). Whose vision and whose voice? Setting the school improvement agenda *with* students, not *for* students. *Australian Education Leadership*, *41*(3), 40–42.

Wilkinson, R., & Pickett, K. (2019). *The inner level: How more equal societies reduce stress, restore sanity, and improve everyone's well-being*. London, UK: Penguin Press.

Williams, J. (2019). *Stand out of our light: Freedom and resistance in the attention economy*. New York, NY: Cambridge University Press.

Wilson, D. S. (2019) *This view of life*. New York, NY: Pantheon.

Wilson, E. O. (2014). *The meaning of human existence*. New York, NY: W. W. Norton.

Index

Acknowledgments

From both Michael and Mary Jean

We want to start with Corwin—publishers par excellence. And of course, it is because of the individuals and the team that we are so grateful. Of special note is senior editor Arnis Burvikovs, who is retiring as this book gets published. We are proud to be one of his last births and so fortunate to have been a recipient of the many books, guidance, creativity, wisdom, and timely and brilliant ideas he has fashioned in publishing Fullan's books over the years. He is irreplaceable and loved by us and by many others. And the team: Desirée Bartlett, Eliza Erickson, Melanie Birdsall, Ariel Curry, and those at the helm: Lisa Shaw, who just retired, and Mike Soules. All a comprehensive joy to work with!

With respect to the ideas in the book, there is no way we could thank all those who contributed over the years. We spend most of our time with practitioners, and what we have learned is impossible to trace. Certainly, we have gained a great deal in our immersive work in Ontario, California, and Victoria, Australia—but really found friendships and knowledge worldwide. Our work across Canada has also been a source of pride including working with the Chagnon Foundation in Quebec where our books are published *en français*.

Our "applied" research colleagues are invaluable and we dare not try to list them. Our team—using the term widely as we mix and match on many fronts—is brilliant and endlessly resourceful: Joanne Quinn, Bill Hogarth, Eleanor Adam, Mag Gardner, and Max Drummy; several were specifically helpful for the ideas in this book—Davis Campbell, Jean Clinton, Claudia Cuttress, Santiago Rincón-Gallardo, and Bruce Armstrong. We feel guilty even providing a list because there are so many others around the world in our work on "system coherence" and "new pedagogies for deep learning."

From Michael

On a personal note Andy Hargreaves has been a powerful soulmate. Dalton McGuinty on the political front when we cut our teeth on systemwide reform in Ontario from 2003 to 2013. I never learned so much. My family who I have been closer to in the last decade than ever before: Wendy—a chameleon of tough and soft whenever the environment calls for it; the older children, Chris, Maureen, and Josh are ever closer, even on the professional front where Josh's "Maximum City" innovation is right in our wheelhouse. The two "younger" boys are flourishing—Bailey, who now works with me, learning a mile a minute, and Conor, on the move in many ways including ever degrees of closeness to his fiancée, Michelle. And the grandchildren: Danny, Peter, Maddie, and Jake, who was born two days ago as I write this.

Finally, my co-author, Mary Jean Gallagher—talk about learning together. We have held hands with the devil and lived to tell about it—this book!

From Mary Jean

This is my first book, and I have learned so much on so many fronts, it is difficult to acknowledge my many guides along my path of learning. Several though stand out for having believed in my capabilities long before I did and who were both patient and impatient as I moved along: Sue Zanin throughout my career, Sharon Taylor for teaching me to be brave, Lorna Earl for planting the seed, and several colleagues in Ontario as we dreamed and worked together for a better way—Eleanor Newman, Richard Franz, and Mike Jancik to name but a few and Mark Brear from Victoria who challenged me to reflect more deeply on system improvement in different environments. I want to acknowledge the love and support of my family: Bob, who was always ready to convince me I could do much that I would not have dared to dream about—leading, flying, taking career risks, and writing this book to identify just a few—and who matched his belief in me with his very best professional and personal advice and protective love, and our daughter Michelle, whose constant encouragement, energy, wry feedback, and laughter brings sunshine to every day. She is wise, loving, learning, and leading herself now, getting stronger as a professional as well; her thoughtful reflections and observations illuminate my path as I do hers.

And to my co-author, Michael Fullan—learning together indeed. You are an amazing mentor: you helped convince Dalton McGuinty to trust me to lead; your writing, thinking, and advice shaped my understanding of change leadership and being open to learning over decades of my career, and it is my great privilege to work as part of your team and in particular as co-author of this book. You have been generous with your knowledge and far more patient than I had any right to expect. Thank you.

About the Authors

Michael Fullan (OC) is the former dean of the Ontario Institute for Studies in Education and professor emeritus of the University of Toronto. He is co-leader of the New Pedagogies for Deep Learning global initiative (www.npdl .global). Recognized as a worldwide authority on educational reform, he advises policymakers, local leaders, and school communities in helping to achieve the moral purpose of all children's learning. He served as Premier Dalton McGuinty's special policy adviser in Ontario from 2003 to 2013, and he was part of Premier Kathleen Wynne's advisory team from 2013 to 2018. Fullan received the Order of Canada (OC) in December 2012. He holds five honorary doctorates from universities around the world.

Fullan is a prolific award-winning author whose books have been published in many languages. Learning Forward gave Fullan the 2002 Book of the Year Award for *Leading in a Culture of Change*—a book that he revised and updated as a second edition appearing January 2020. Andy Hargreaves and Michael Fullan's book *Professional Capital* received the Grawemeyer Award in 2015.

Fullan's latest books are *Coherence: The Right Drivers in Action for Schools, Districts, and Systems* (with Joanne Quinn); *Deep Learning: Engage the World Change the World* (with Joanne Quinn and Joanne McEachen); *Dive Into Deep Learning: Tools for Engagement* (with Joanne Quinn, Joanne McEachen, Mag Gardner, and Max Drummy); *Surreal*

Change (autobiography); *Core Governance* (with Davis Campbell); and *Nuance: Why Some Leaders Succeed and Others Fail.*

Fullan's most recent work in deep learning focuses on linking learning, engagement, and well-being on a large scale as a force for individual and societal improvement.

For more information on books, articles, videos, or podcasts, please go to www.michaefullan.ca.

Bob Gallagher

Mary Jean Gallagher is a lifelong educator and leader with a passion for improved learning and teaching. She is the former chief student achievement officer and assistant deputy minister of student achievement for the province of Ontario, Canada. In that role she led the implementation of Ontario's education reforms. Prior to the Ministry, she served as director (superintendent) of education of Canada's southernmost school district, the Greater Essex County District School Board, and its predecessor, since 1995 and has also served as chair of the Council of Ontario Directors of Education, CEO of the Ontario Education Improvement Commission, a secondary school principal, and a school superintendent of staffing and development.

Gallagher is recognized as an expert in educational reform and implementation and is currently named a Critical Friend to the Department of Education for the state of Victoria, Australia. She has provided presentations and advice to ministries and departments of education, school districts, and educational organizations in 27 countries on six continents. Gallagher has authored a number of articles on system reform in education and holds an Honorary Doctor of Laws Degree from the University of Windsor. She was named Outstanding Educator of the Year by the Ontario Phi Delta Kappan Association in 2013 and the Ontario Principals' Council in 2015. In 2016, the Learning Partnership of Canada recognized her as Canada's Outstanding Education Leader.

For more information, see www.mjgallagher.ca.

A SAGE Publishing Company

Helping educators make the greatest impact

CORWIN HAS ONE MISSION: to enhance education through intentional professional learning.

We build long-term relationships with our authors, educators, clients, and associations who partner with us to develop and continuously improve the best evidence-based practices that establish and support lifelong learning.

Leadership That Makes an Impact

LYN SHARRATT

Explore 14 essential parameters to guide system and school leaders toward building powerful collaborative learning cultures.

MICHAEL FULLAN

How do you break the cycle of surface-level change to tackle complex challenges? *Nuance* is the answer.

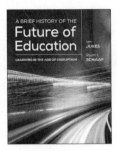

IAN JUKES & RYAN L. SCHAAF

The digital environment has radically changed how students need to learn. Get ready to be challenged to accommodate today's learners.

ERIC SHENINGER

Lead for efficacy in these disruptive times! Cultivating school culture focused on the achievement of students while anticipating change is imperative.

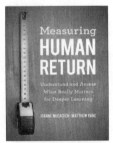

JOANNE MCEACHEN & MATTHEW KANE

Getting at the heart of what matters for students is key to deeper learning that connects with their lives.

LEE G. BOLMAN & TERRENCE E. DEAL

Sometimes all it takes to solve a problem is to reframe it by listening to wise advice from a trusted mentor.

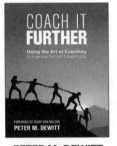

PETER M. DEWITT

This go-to guide is written for coaches, leaders looking to be coached, and leaders interested in coaching burgeoning leaders.

ANTHONY KIM & ALEXIS GONZALES-BLACK

Designed to foster flexibility and continuous innovation, this resource expands cutting-edge management and organizational techniques to empower schools with the agility and responsiveness vital to their new environment.

To order your copies, visit **corwin.com/leadership**

Also Available

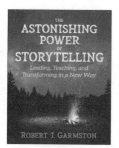

ROBERT J. GARMSTON

Stories have unique power to captivate and motivate action. This guidebook shows how to leverage storytelling to engage students.

JOYCE L. EPSTEIN

Strengthen programs of family and community engagement to promote equity and increase student success!

DEAN T. SPAULDING & GAIL M. SMITH

Help teams navigate the world of data analysis for ongoing school improvement with an easy-to-follow framework that dives deep into data-driven instruction.

KENNETH LEITHWOOD

By drawing on the numerous cases and stories, educators will gain a deep understanding of how to prepare the next wave of talented school leaders for success.

ANGELINE A. ANDERSON, SUSAN K. BORG, & STEPHANIE L. EDGAR

Centered on teacher voice and grounded in foundations of collaboration and data-informed planning, Transform Academy comes to life through its stories, and accompanying action steps.

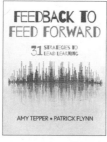

AMY TEPPER & PATRICK FLYNN

Leaders know that feedback is essential to teacher development. This how-to guide helps leaders conduct comprehensive observations, analyze lessons, develop high-leverage action steps, and craft effective feedback.

MICHAEL FULLAN, JOANNE QUINN, & JOANNE MCEACHEN

This book defines what deep learning is, and takes up the question of how to mobilize complex whole-system change.

JOANNE QUINN, JOANNE MCEACHEN, MICHAEL FULLAN, MAG GARDNER, & MAX DRUMMY

This resource shows you how to design deep learning, measure progress, and assess the conditions to sustain innovation and mobilization.